THE USBORNE
INTERNET-LINKED
LIBRARY OF SCIENCE
ENERGY, FORCES
& MOTION

Usborne Publishing has made every
effort to ensure that material on the sites
recommended is suitable for its intended
purpose, and the sites are regularly reviewed by
Usborne editors. However, the content of a website
may change at any time, and Usborne Publishing is not
responsible for the accuracy or suitability of the information
on any website other than its own. We recommend that
children are supervised while on the Internet, that they do not
use Internet chat rooms, and that you use Internet filtering
software to block unsuitable material.

First published in 2001 by Usborne Publishing Ltd,
Usborne House, 83-85 Saffron Hill, London EC1N 8RT, England.

www.usborne.com

Printed in Spain

THE USBORNE
INTERNET-LINKED
LIBRARY OF SCIENCE
ENERGY, FORCES & MOTION

Alastair Smith and Corinne Henderson

Designed by Ruth Russell, Karen Tomlins,
Jane Rigby and Adam Constantine

Digital illustrations by Verinder Bhachu
Digital imagery by Joanne Kirkby

Edited by Laura Howell
Cover design: Nicola Butler
Consultant: Dr Tom Petersen
Web site adviser: Lisa Watts
Editorial assistant: Valerie Modd

Managing designer: Ruth Russell
Managing editor: Judy Tatchell

INTERNET LINKS

Throughout this book, we have suggested websites where you can find out more about energy, forces and motion. Here are some of the things you can do on the recommended sites:

- design your own rollercoaster ride
- test your knowledge of friction by saving an animated skydiver from a messy fate
- land a virtual spacecraft successfully on the surface of different planets
- find out how much you weigh on any planet

USBORNE QUICKLINKS

To visit the sites in this book, go to the Usborne Quicklinks Website, where you'll find links to take you to all the sites. Just go to **www.usborne-quicklinks.com** and enter the keywords "science energy".

The links in Usborne Quicklinks are regularly reviewed and updated, but occasionally you may get a message that a site is unavailable. This might be temporary, so try again later, or even the next day. If any of the sites close down, we will, if possible, replace them with suitable alternatives, so you will always find an up-to-date list of sites in Usborne Quicklinks.

WHAT YOU NEED

Some websites need additional free programs, called plug-ins, to play sounds, or to show videos, animations or 3-D images. A message will appear on your screen if a site needs a particular plug-in. There is usually a button on the site that you can click on to download it. Alternatively, go to **www.usborne-quicklinks.com** and click on "Net Help". There you can find links to download plug-ins.

INTERNET SAFETY

When using the Internet, please make sure you follow these guidelines:

- Ask your parent's or guardian's permission before you connect to the Internet.

- If a website asks you to enter your name, address, email address, telephone number or any other personal details, ask permission from an adult before you type anything.

- If you receive an email from someone you don't know, tell an adult and do not reply to the email.

- Never arrange to meet with anyone you have talked to on the Internet.

NOTES FOR PARENTS

The websites described in this book are regularly reviewed and the links in Usborne Quicklinks are updated. However, the content of a website may change at any time and Usborne Publishing is not responsible for the content on any website other than its own. We recommend that children are supervised while on the Internet, that they do not use Internet Chat Rooms, and that you use Internet filtering software to block unsuitable material. Please ensure that your children read and follow the safety guidelines printed above. For more information, see the "Net Help" area on the Usborne Quicklinks website.

DOWNLOADABLE PICTURES

Pictures in this book marked with a ★ symbol may be downloaded from Usborne Quicklinks for your own personal use, for example, to illustrate a homework report or project. The pictures are the copyright of Usborne Publishing and may not be used for any commercial or profit-related purpose.

www.usborne-quicklinks.com

Go to Usborne Quicklinks and enter the keywords "science energy" for:
- direct links to all the websites in this book
- free downloadable pictures, which appear throughout this book marked with a ★ symbol

SEE FOR YOURSELF

The *See for yourself* boxes in this book contain experiments, activities or observations which we have tested. Some recommended websites also contain experiments, but we have not tested all of these. This book will be used by readers of different ages and abilities, so it is important that you do not tackle an experiment on your own, either from the book or the Web, that involves equipment that you do not normally use, such as a kitchen knife or cooker. Instead, ask an adult to help you.

CONTENTS

ENERGY, FORCES AND MOTION

Physics is the branch of science that deals with matter and energy, the forces that act in the universe, and the results that these forces produce. For instance, when you kick a football, energy is used to create a force on the ball, which in turn produces motion. This book explains many aspects of energy, forces and motion, and the physical laws which govern them.

These balloons float upwards because they are filled with hot air, which always rises. As the air inside them cools, the force of gravity pulls the balloons back down to the ground.

ENERGY

Without energy, nothing could live or grow, and there would be no movement, light, heat or noise. Energy can take many different forms: heat, light and sound are all different forms of energy. For anything to happen, energy is needed, and whenever anything happens, energy is converted from one form to another.

The energy from the Sun is about equal to that supplied by one million million million large power stations.

FORMS OF ENERGY

Energy can exist in many forms and the different forms make different things happen. As well as heat, light and sound, there are other forms such as chemical energy, kinetic energy and potential energy.

Chemical energy is energy that is released during chemical reactions. Batteries, food, and fuels such as coal, oil and petrol, are stores of chemical energy.

The energy used to move this hammer comes from food eaten and stored in the body of the person using the hammer. Chemical energy is released from the food by reactions in the body cells.

Potential energy is the energy an object has because it is in a position where it is affected by a force, such as magnetism* or gravity*. Objects that can be stretched or squashed, such as elastic bands and springs, have **elastic potential energy** or **strain energy**.

The higher the hammer, the greater its potential energy.

Moving objects have **kinetic energy**, the energy of movement. The faster something moves, the more kinetic energy it has. As it slows down, it loses kinetic energy.

The moving hammer transfers kinetic energy to the nail, which moves into the wood.

* Gravity, 32; Magnetism, 59.

ENERGY CONVERSION

The **law of conservation of energy** states that energy can never be created or destroyed. Whenever anything happens, energy is converted into a different form. This is what happens, for example, when plants use energy from sunlight to make food, and when animals eat them in turn.

Example of energy conversion

1. Plant uses energy from sunlight to make food.

2. Plant stores food as chemical energy.

3. Hummingbird feeds on plant. Chemical energy is converted to kinetic energy and some heat energy when bird moves.

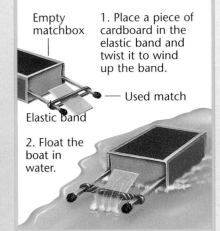

★

Chemical energy in batteries is changed to electrical energy in a flashlight.

Electrical energy is changed to light and heat energy in the bulb.

ENERGY CHAINS

An **energy chain** is a way of showing how energy is converted from one form to another. The pictures on the right show the energy changes that take place in a power station, where the chemical energy in coal is converted into electrical energy.

A coal-fired power station

The final forms in most energy chains are heat and light. Even this energy is not lost, but it spreads out into the environment and is very difficult to harness for any useful purpose.

* Turbines, 49.

Energy conversion in a power station

Coal is the fossilized remains of plants that grew long ago. It is a chemical store of energy that came originally from the Sun.

When the coal is burned, the chemical energy is converted to heat energy, which is used to heat water to make steam.

The steam turns turbines*. This produces kinetic energy – the energy of movement.

The kinetic energy is converted to electrical energy in a device called a **generator**.

Appliances such as lamps, televisions, heaters and audio equipment convert electrical energy into light, heat and sound.

★

See for yourself

In this matchbox paddle-boat, the elastic potential energy stored by a twisted elastic band is changed into kinetic energy that moves the boat forwards.

Empty matchbox

1. Place a piece of cardboard in the elastic band and twist it to wind up the band.

— Used match

Elastic band

2. Float the boat in water.

Internet links

Go to **www.usborne-quicklinks.com** for links to the following websites:

Website 1 Try a quiz about energy and find out more about sources of energy, with games and animations.

Website 2 See if you can make some energy chains in an online activity.

Website 3 Animations about types of energy and other energy concepts.

Website 4 Find out about energy and the Earth, with quizzes and games.

Websites 5-6 Take a virtual tour of a power plant and see how electricity is generated and distributed, with diagrams.

ENERGY RESOURCES

Energy is used to heat and light houses, to cook food and provide the power for factories and cars. This energy can be obtained by burning fuels, or by harnessing the power of, say, the wind, the Sun, or moving water.

About half the people of the world burn wood, dung or charcoal to provide the energy that they need for cooking and heating.

Wood, coal, oil and natural gas are called **non-renewable fuels** because they can be used only once. Other sources of energy, such as the Sun, wind and water, are called **renewable energy resources** because they generate power without being used up themselves.

ENERGY USAGE

The pie chart below shows the percentages of the different power resources that are used to provide energy for homes and industry.

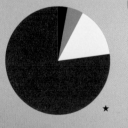

- ■ Nuclear energy* 3%
- ■ Renewable energy 5%
- □ Wood 15%
- ★ ■ Fossil fuels 77%

This wind turbine uses the power of the wind to provide energy. The turning motion of the massive blades is transformed into electricity in a generator, which is in a box just behind the blades.

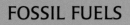

FOSSIL FUELS

Coal, oil and natural gas are called **fossil fuels** because they formed from the fossilized remains of plants or animals. Over 20% of the world's energy comes from coal. When fossil fuels burn, they release carbon dioxide and other gases into the air and they are partly to blame for problems such as acid rain and the greenhouse effect*.

Here you can see the fossilized remains of a prehistoric plant in a lump of coal.

RENEWABLE ENERGY

Only 5% of the world's energy comes from renewable energy resources. Two examples of these are shown below, while another, solar energy, is explained on the opposite page.

Hydroelectric power

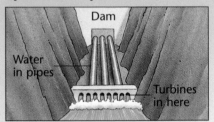

Water stored behind a dam is released through pipes. As it gushes down, it turns turbines, which generate electricity. This is hydroelectric power.

Biogas

When organic matter, such as animal waste, rots, it produces burnable gases, known as biogases. Burning biogas can produce heat for buildings and water.

* Greenhouse effect, 59; Nuclear energy, 18.

SOLAR ENERGY

Energy from the Sun is called **solar energy**. It consists of heat and light energy, both of which move in the form of electromagnetic waves*. It can be used to produce electricity with a device called a **solar cell**, or to heat water using **solar collectors**.

In a solar collector, heat from the Sun is absorbed by the black absorber panel, which heats the water in the pipes.

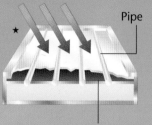

Sun's rays

★

Pipe

Absorber panel

Cutaway diagram of a roof with a solar heating system. The hot water is for domestic use, such as washing, and also for the central heating system.

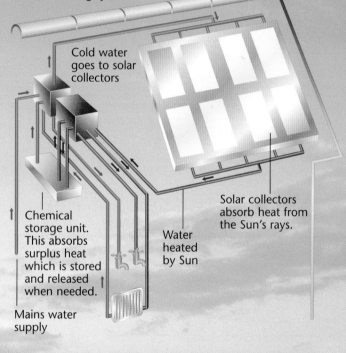

★

Cold water goes to solar collectors

Chemical storage unit. This absorbs surplus heat which is stored and released when needed.

Mains water supply

Water heated by Sun

Solar collectors absorb heat from the Sun's rays.

ENERGY EFFICIENCY

Machines take one form of energy, for example, electricity, and change it into another form of energy. Machines are described as efficient if they change most of the energy that is used to power them, into the useful form of energy that is needed.

Energy-saving fluorescent tube lights are more efficient than normal light bulbs because they turn more electrical energy into light and waste less as heat.

MEASURING ENERGY

Energy is measured using units called **joules (J)**. One thousand joules is a **kilojoule (kJ)**. The foods that you eat give you varying amounts of energy.

An ordinary sized apple (100g) contains 150kJ of chemical energy. The same mass of chocolate contains 2,335kJ.

Power is the energy used in a certain time and it is measured in units called **watts (W)**. One watt is equal to one joule per second. The more energy a machine produces in a certain period of time, the more powerful it is.

A 60 watt light bulb uses 60 joules of energy each second. A 100 watt bulb uses 100 joules per second and produces more heat and light energy.

100 watt light bulb

60 watt light bulb

See for yourself

On a hot day you can see how the Sun's energy heats things up. Coil a garden hose so that as much of it as possible is in sunlight. Attach it to a water supply and turn it on so that water comes out. Then turn off the water and block up the end of the pipe using, say, a cork. Leave it in the sun for an hour.

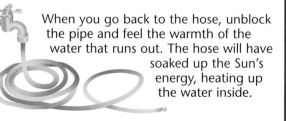

When you go back to the hose, unblock the pipe and feel the warmth of the water that runs out. The hose will have soaked up the Sun's energy, heating up the water inside.

Internet links

Go to **www.usborne-quicklinks.com** for links to the following websites:

Website 1 Explore a clickable picture to find useful definitions of different types of renewable energy.

Website 2 A site from the California Energy Commission with lots of useful information and fun activities related to energy.

Website 3 Watch animations that show how coal, oil and gas formed and how solar, tidal and wind power work.

Website 4 Simple introduction and quiz on renewable and non-renewable energy.

Website 5 Take a virtual tour of an alternative technology centre and see how many energy-saving ideas you can find.

* Electromagnetic radiation, 58.

Heat is a form of energy that flows from one place to another because of a difference in temperatur Temperature is a measure of how hot something is.

HEAT ENERGY

When a substance absorbs heat, its **internal energy** increases. Internal energy is made up of two types of energy. Firstly, there is the kinetic energy* of the particles as they move about in the substance. Secondly, there is the potential energy* of the particles, ready to be used.

This red-hot river of liquid rock was formed when rocks inside the Earth absorbed so much heat that they melted.

Ice in water

Heat energy flows from hot objects to cooler ones and continues to flow until they reach the same temperature. For example, water that has ice in it loses heat energy to the ice, which gains heat energy. Eventually, all the water molecules (from the water and the ice) reach the same temperature.

MEASURING HEAT ENERGY

Like all forms of energy, heat is measured in **joules (J)**, named after the English scientist James Joule (1818-89). He was the first to recognize that heat is a form of energy. Using a contraption like the one below, Joule showed how potential energy lost by the falling weights was gained by the water in the form of heat energy, as its temperature rose.

Joule's experiment

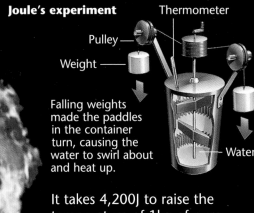

Thermometer
Pulley
Weight

Falling weights made the paddles in the container turn, causing the water to swirl about and heat up.

Water

It takes 4,200J to raise the temperature of 1kg of pure water by just 1°C.

* Kinetic energy, Potential energy, 8.

HEAT AND EXPANSION

Most substances expand wher they are heated because, as their particles vibrate more vigorously, they push each other further apart. Gases and most liquids expand more thar solids because their molecules have more energy to break free of the forces that hold them together.

Different solids expand at different rates. This can be seer in a **bimetallic strip**, a strip of copper and iron fixed firmly together. When heated, the copper expands more than the iron, so the strip bends.

Bimetallic strips are used in **thermostats** – devices that switch an electrical circuit on and off in response to a change in temperature.

Bimetallic strip in a thermostat

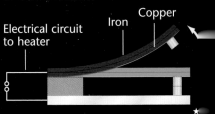

Iron   Copper
Electrical circuit
to heater

See for yourself

Take a jar of dried peas or beans and shake it gently. The contents vibrate but stay in roughly the same places. This is what happens to the particles in a solid when they are heated a little.

If you put the same amount of heat into two different substances, their temperatures change by different amounts. The substances are said to have different **thermal** (or **specific heat**) **capacities**.

Oil and water, for example, have different specific heat capacities.

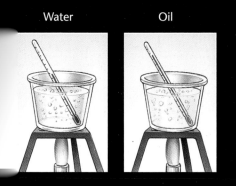

Water   Oil

The same amount of heat makes oil hotter than water.

The different thermal capacities of the land and the sea cause sea breezes. In the day, the land heats up faster than the sea. Warm air over the land rises and cooler air blows in from the sea.

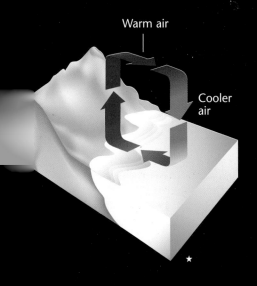

Warm air

Cooler air

Coastal wind patterns like this one develop mostly during spells of warm weather.

Temperature can be measured in degrees Celsius (°C) or Fahrenheit (°F), or on the absolute temperature scale.

The **Celsius scale** has two fixed points: ice point (0°C) and steam point (100°C). Each Celsius degree is one hundredth of the difference between these two points.

212°F	100°C
200°F	
190°F	90°C
180°F	80°C
170°F	
160°F	70°C
150°F	
140°F	60°C
130°F	
120°F	50°C
110°F	
100°F	40°C
90°F	30°C
80°F	
70°F	20°C
60°F	
50°F	10°C
40°F	
32°F	0°C

An early Celsius thermometer ★

The Celsius and Fahrenheit scales ★

In the **Fahrenheit scale**, the values 32°F and 212°F are given to the ice and steam points. There are 180 degrees between them.

The **absolute temperature scale** is measured in units called **kelvins (K)**, which are the same size as degrees Celsius. The scale starts at a point called **absolute zero** (zero K) which is the same as -273°C. This is the temperature at which no more energy can be removed from a substance.

A **thermometer** is an instrument for measuring temperature. It may contain a liquid that expands when heated, or a wire whose resistance to electric current changes if the temperature changes.

Liquid in glass thermometers contain mercury or, for measuring very low temperatures, alcohol.

Constriction stops liquid returning to the bulb before a reading is taken.

Maximum and **minimum thermometers** contain pointers that record the highest or lowest temperature reached.

| 35 | 36 | 37 | 38 | 39 | 40 |

Liquid crystal thermometers contain liquid crystals that change colour when heated.

Digital thermometers contain an electronic component that is sensitive to heat. It shows the temperature on a digital display.

Internet links

Go to **www.usborne-quicklinks.com** for links to the following websites:

Website 1 Find out more about heat, with simple experiments.

Website 2 Review the principles of heat energy, with animated examples.

Website 3 How thermometers work.

Website 4 See a virtual reconstruction of James Joule's heat experiment.

HEAT TRANSFER

Heat can be transferred from one place to another by convection, conduction or radiation.

CONVECTION

Convection is the main way in which heat energy is transferred in liquids and gases. When a liquid or gas is heated, the part nearest the heat source expands and becomes less dense*, so it rises. The cooler, denser liquid sinks. Movements like this in liquids or gases are called **convection currents**.

The pattern of winds around the Earth are caused by convection currents. These occur because more of the Sun's energy hits the surface near the equator. As the air is heated, it expands and rises and colder, denser air rushes in, creating a wind.

— Warm air rises.

— Air cools and sinks.

Fridges are kept cold by convection currents. Cool air near the top of the fridge sinks, while warmer air rises to be cooled.

Glider plane takes spiral path upwards.

★

Convection currents in the atmosphere lift glider.

Convection currents are carrying clouds of ash from this volcano into the upper atmosphere.

See for yourself

Gently drop a small feather or piece of tissue paper above a warm radiator. See which way the feather or paper floats.

The radiator heats the air above it, causing the air to rise and form a convection current. If it is light enough, the feather or paper will be carried upwards on the convection current.

* Density, 40.

CONDUCTION

Conduction is the way in which heat energy in a solid is transferred. The energy of the particles nearest to the heat source increases. These particles vibrate and pass on some of their energy, spreading heat through the substance.

A desert fox has large ears which help it to keep cool. Excess heat is transferred from its ears to the air by conduction and spreads away by convection.

Metals are good **conductors** because, as well as their vibrating particles, they contain freely moving electrons*. These carry heat energy around more quickly than the vibrations alone. Substances that conduct heat slowly, such as wood and water, are called **insulators**. Air is a good insulator and so are materials that trap air, such as wool, fur and feathers.

Metal heats up quickly as it is a very good conductor of heat.

Heat spreads quickly through metal particles.

Fat and feathers insulate birds such as penguins, helping to keep them warm.

RADIATION

Heat transfer by **radiation** refers to energy that moves in the form of electromagnetic waves*.

The Sun's radiation travels at 300 million metres per second. It takes about eight minutes to reach the Earth.

Sun's heat

Radiation does not depend on particle movement, and is the only form of energy that can cross a **vacuum** (a space completely empty of matter). All types of radiation, for instance light rays, cause things to heat up, but **infrared radiation** is the type which causes the greatest temperature rise.

The Sun sends out infrared radiation, as do hot objects, such as fires and light bulbs. Dark-coloured objects absorb the radiation, while light ones reflect it, and stay cool.

In Antarctica, the snow reflects over 90% of the radiation from the Sun back into the atmosphere. The surface receives very little heat, so the air remains cold.

Radiation

Snow reflects the Sun's radiation.

VACUUM FLASKS

A **vacuum flask** is a container for keeping liquids at a constant temperature. It is made up of two glass containers, one inside the other, with a vacuum between them. The vacuum prevents the transfer of heat by conduction or convection (see left). Very shiny surfaces reduce the amount of heat transferred by radiation.

Vacuum flask

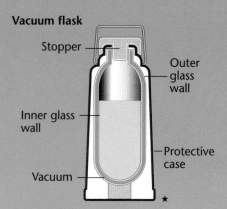

Stopper

Outer glass wall

Inner glass wall

Protective case

Vacuum

★

Internet links

Go to **www.usborne-quicklinks.com** for links to the following websites:

Website 1 Useful information about temperature.

Website 2 Find out how refrigerators and vacuum flasks work.

Website 3 Explore an infrared photo album.

Website 4 Learn more about insulation with an experiment to keep a mummy's tomb cool.

Website 5 Do heat and temperature experiments in an online lab.

Electromagnetic radiation, Electron, 58.

RADIOACTIVITY

All matter is made of particles called **atoms**. Every atom contains a **nucleus** which is made up of **protons** and **neutrons**. Nuclei hold vast amounts of energy, called **nuclear energy**. Some substances are **radioactive**. This means that their atoms release some of this energy as radiation*. This can be dangerous to living things, but can be used in many ways.

Nucleus—

Beta particles are very high-energy electrons emitted when a neutron in the nucleus decays.

Alpha particles are clusters containing two protons and two neutrons.

TYPES OF RADIATION

When a substance is radioactive, it is said to be **unstable**. The atoms become stable by losing some of their nuclear energy as radiation.

The type of radiation that the atoms give out is either **alpha**, **beta** or **gamma radiation**. The first two are streams of particles. The last takes the form of **gamma rays**, which are an extremely powerful form of electromagnetic waves*.

The Greek letters below are used to describe the different types of radiation.

Alpha   Beta   Gamma

A nucleus first throws off either alpha or beta particles, and then, if it has extra energy, gamma radiation.

The three nuclei shown on this page are all unstable. Each nucleus is emitting a different type of radiation.

Alpha particles move slowly and are stopped by any substance thicker than paper. They are identical to the nuclei of helium atoms and scientists think helium is created by natural radioactivity in the Earth. Beta particles are more penetrating than alpha particles and many move almost at the speed of light. Gamma rays are the most penetrating.

Range of radioactive particles

Symbol for radioactive substances

Alpha particles travel less than 10cm in air and are absorbed by thick paper.

Beta particles have a range of 1m in air and are absorbed by 1mm of copper.

The intensity of gamma rays is halved by 13mm of lead or by about 120m of air.

★

Gamma rays are very high-energy electromagnetic waves that move at the speed of light.

★

* Electromagnetic radiation, 58; Radiation, 15.

USES OF RADIATION

In industry, radiation is used to check the thickness of sheets of paper and plastic. Tiny irregularities can be detected by measuring the amount of beta radiation that passes through the sheets. Food, such as fruit and meat, can be irradiated with gamma rays, and this keeps it fresh.

After two weeks, these irradiated strawberries are still fresh.

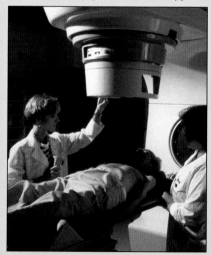

In hospitals, doctors use **radioactive tracing** to follow a substance through a patient's body. For example, to see how a patient's body deals with sugar, they can attach some radioactive carbon-14 to molecules of sugar and track the radiation given off by the carbon-14.

Radiotherapy uses carefully controlled doses of radiation to kill cancer cells, which are living cells that are growing in a disorderly way.

A patient being given radiotherapy

RADIOACTIVE DECAY

After ejecting particles, a nucleus becomes the nucleus of a different element. This is called **radioactive decay**. If the new element is also unstable, the process of decay will continue until there are atoms with stable nuclei.

For example, when the unstable radioactive substance plutonium-242 gives off an alpha particle (which consists of two protons and two neutrons), it becomes uranium-238. The diagram below shows how plutonium decays to become uranium and then thorium.

The numbers written in front of the symbol for the substance are the mass number (top) and atomic number (bottom). The **mass number** is the number of neutrons and protons in a nucleus. The **atomic number** is just the number of protons.

Radioactive decay of plutonium

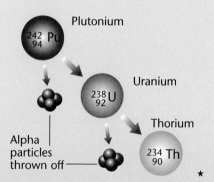

Plutonium
$^{242}_{94}Pu$

Uranium
$^{238}_{92}U$

Thorium
$^{234}_{90}Th$

Alpha particles thrown off

The length of time it takes for the nuclei of an element to decay is measured by its **half-life**. This is the time taken for half of the nuclei in a sample to decay. Every element has a different half-life. Radium-221 has a half-life of 30 seconds. Uranium-238 has a half-life of 4,500,000,000 years.

CARBON DATING

Carbon dating is a method of calculating the time that has passed since living matter died. All living things contain a small amount of carbon-14, which has a half-life of 5,700 years. When living things die, the carbon-14 decays. The age of the remains can be calculated by measuring how much radiation is still being given off.

Carbon dating showed that this insect was trapped in amber resin five thousand years ago.

DANGER!

Radioactive substances are transported in thick lead containers to prevent radiation from escaping. Exposure to radiation can cause burns, cataracts and cancer.

Robots are used to handle dangerous radioactive substances.

Internet links

Go to **www.usborne-quicklinks.com** for links to the following websites:

Website 1 A very useful site about nuclear science.

Website 2 Explore the website of the European Organization for Nuclear Research (CERN).

Website 3 Helpful online lessons about radiation, with online tests.

Website 4 Review all aspects of radiation, including safety and uses.

Websites 5-6 Useful information and animations about radiation and its hazards and uses.

NUCLEAR POWER

Nuclear energy can be harnessed, using controlled nuclear reactions, to produce power for industrial and home use. It can also be released, in an extremely violent way, when nuclear weapons explode.

NUCLEAR REACTIONS

There are two types of nuclear reactions: **nuclear fusion** and **nuclear fission**. Fusion means "joining" and during nuclear fusion, two small nuclei combine to form a larger one. Nuclear fusion only takes place at extremely high temperatures and releases huge amounts of energy.

Nuclear fusion

Two nuclei join to form one large one.

Fission means "splitting apart" and nuclear fission occurs when the nucleus of an atom is bombarded with neutrons*. The nucleus splits open, releasing neutrons and large amounts of energy. This process takes place inside nuclear reactors (see opposite page).

Nuclear fission

A nucleus splits open, forming two or more new nuclei.

The dust created by this nuclear explosion is highly radioactive*. It contaminates everything on which it falls.

NUCLEAR WEAPONS

Nuclear weapons produce uncontrolled nuclear reactions. The energy is released in massive explosions. **Atomic bombs** use nuclear fission reactions. **Hydrogen bombs** use nuclear fusion. In World War II, the USA dropped atomic bombs on the cities of Hiroshima and Nagasaki in Japan, killing many thousands of people.

World War II atomic bomb

Radioactive* plutonium in here

* Neutrons, Radioactivity, 16.

NUCLEAR REACTORS

The energy released by controlled fission reactions can be used to generate electricity, and to power submarines and aircraft carriers.

Nuclear-powered submarine

Engine room

Reactor

Such reactions take place in **nuclear reactors**, such as the pressurized water reactor shown in the diagram at the bottom of the page.

Inside a nuclear reactor, rods made of a radioactive substance such as uranium are bombarded with neutrons*. The nuclei split up, releasing radiation and more neutrons, which set up a chain reaction.

Nuclear power stations generate lots of electricity. However, the used fuel rods remain dangerously radioactive for thousands of years. Disposing of them safely is very difficult.

Nuclear power station

PRESSURIZED WATER REACTOR

A **pressurized water reactor** is one type of nuclear reactor found in power stations. The energy released in the core of the reactor is used to heat water to make steam. The steam turns turbines* that generate electricity.

Nuclear fission reactions take place in the core of the nuclear reactor (1).

The energy released heats pressurized water in the primary water circuit (2).

Heat from the primary water circuit heats the water in the secondary circuit to make steam (3).

Uranium rod

(2)

Steam (3)

(1)

(4)

Generator

Steam-driven turbines (4) generate electricity.

Steam is cooled in the condenser (5) by a supply of water.

(5)

Pump

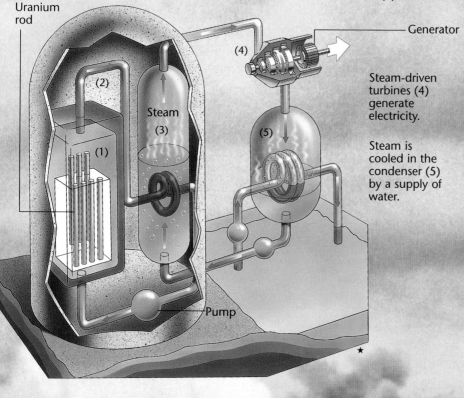

SAFETY FIRST

Nuclear reactions are dangerous to living things. To prevent accidents which would pollute land and air with radiation, the workings in power stations are monitored closely.

Dangerous processes inside a nuclear power station are carefully monitored.

Internet links

Go to www.usborne-quicklinks.com for links to the following websites:

Website 1 Illustrated guide to nuclear energy, nuclear reactors and much more.

Website 2 Animated explanation and tour of a nuclear power station.

Website 3 Animated facts and activities about nuclear power.

Website 4 Here you'll find a timeline of nuclear technology.

Website 5 Take part in a virtual debate on the pros and cons of nuclear energy.

* Neutrons, 16; Turbines, 49.

FORCES

A **force** is any push or pull on an object. When you pick up an object, you are exerting a force on it. If you leave it sitting where it is, there are still forces acting on it, but they cancel each other out. Forces can make things move faster or slower, stop, change direction, or change size or shape.

The force of gravity makes these dice fall downwards.

TYPES OF FORCES

Forces affect objects in many different ways. There are forces you can see, such as a foot kicking a ball, and invisible forces, such as magnetism* and gravity*.

The magnetic force which pulls these tacks to the magnet is an invisible force.

You can see the pulling forces at work in a tug of war. The team that pulls with the most force wins.

A single force acting on an object will make it start to move, or move faster or slower. Two equal forces acting in opposite directions try to change the object's size or shape.

Forces that need two or more objects to be touching each other are called **contact forces**. You are using contact forces when you move an object with your hands.

Try rolling one ball into another on a smooth surface. The force of your movement will set the ball rolling. The moving ball will exert a force on the stationary one, causing it to move too.

The surface will exert a force (friction*) on both balls, causing them both to slow down, and eventually stop.

Some forces don't need objects to be touching. The forces that act at a distance include electric force*, magnetism and the force of gravity.

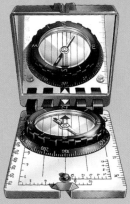

Compasses work because of the Earth's magnetism*.

The contact force of friction* enables pencils to make marks on paper.

When you kick a football, the single force of your kick makes the football start to move.

As you catch a ball, the pushing force of your hands makes the ball slow down and stop.

If you step on a ball, the equal forces of your foot pushing down and the ground pushing up squash it.

* Electric force, 58; Friction, 26; Gravity, 32; Magnetism, 59.

A rollercoaster makes use of lots of different forces to gain speed, twist, turn upside down and race along without flying off the track.

When you are on a rollercoaster, you can feel the different forces acting on your body as you are thrown around.

MEASURING FORCES

The strength of a force is measured in **newtons (N)**, named after the English scientist, Isaac Newton (1642-1727). One newton of force causes a mass of 1kg to accelerate* by one metre per second per second $(1m/s^2)$. This is about the force you would need to lift an empty glass.

A **spring balance** (see right) measures how many newtons a force is exerting. The spring, fixed at one end, is extended (stretched) by the force. **Hooke's law** states that the extension of a material is proportional to the force stretching it. The more the spring stretches, the more newtons the force is applying.

Spring balance

Downward force of weight stretches spring.

The scale gives the strength of the force in newtons.

VECTOR AND SCALAR QUANTITIES

Forces have magnitude (size) and direction. In physics, things that have both these quantities are called **vector quantities**. Acceleration* and velocity* are also vector quantities. A quantity that has magnitude but no direction is called a **scalar quantity**. Temperature, time and mass are examples of scalar quantities. These quantities can be low or high, but they don't have a direction.

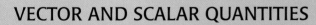

Temperature has only magnitude, so it is a scalar quantity.

Internet links

Go to www.usborne-quicklinks.com for links to the following websites:

Websites 1-2 Explore the physics of forces as you design your own rollercoaster, with useful definitions.

Website 3 Information about forces, including forces involved in skateboarding.

Website 4 Learn how magnetism works - and how to make a compass.

Website 5 Information, animations and a quiz about forces and objects.

Website 6 Find out about forces and what they can do, with online quizzes.

* Acceleration, Velocity, 29.

COMBINING FORCES

There is usually more than one force acting on an object. For example, a sailboard can experience the forces of gravity, the wind, upthrust and waves. The combined effect is a single force called the **resultant force**. If the strength and direction of all forces is known, you can calculate the resultant force and predict what will happen to the object.

Gravity pushes the board down.

Wind in the sail pushes the board this way.

Waves push the board this way.

Resultant force

Upthrust* from the water pushes the board up.

EQUILIBRIUM

There are forces acting on an object even when it is not moving. The forces are all balanced, so they cancel each other out and the object is said to be in **equilibrium**. For example, the force of gravity* pulls down on a tower of cards, while the surface it stands on pushes up with an equal force. The resultant force is zero, so the tower stays in place.

See for yourself

To see forces of equilibrium in action, try building a tower of cards for yourself.

If you knock a card, the forces acting on the structure will no longer be in equilibrium and the tower will collapse.

Making sure that the forces balance is tricky, because each card depends on others to keep it in place. Cards are so flimsy that a slight knock will unbalance them.

* Gravity, 32; Upthrust, 40.

TURNING FORCES

To turn something around a fixed point, for example a door around its hinges, a force with a turning effect is needed. The fixed point is known as a **fulcrum** or **pivot**. It is much easier to turn something around a fulcrum if the force is applied at a distance. This is why a long spanner is more efficient than a shorter one.

It is easiest to undo this bolt by holding the spanner at the end, as the force is then furthest from the fulcrum.

Fulcrum

The force of a turning effect is called a **moment**. The moment around a fulcrum is found by multiplying the strength of the force by its distance from the fulcrum. Moment is measured in **newton metres (Nm)** and can be either clockwise or anticlockwise in direction.

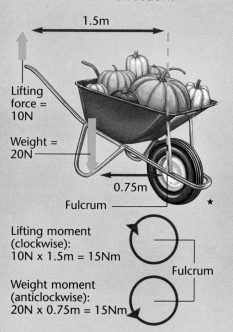

1.5m

Lifting force = 10N

Weight = 20N

0.75m

Fulcrum

Lifting moment (clockwise):
10N x 1.5m = 15Nm

Weight moment (anticlockwise):
20N x 0.75m = 15Nm

Fulcrum

The picture of the wheelbarrow above shows how turning forces can be in equilibrium just like any other forces. The clockwise moment can cancel out the anticlockwise moment.

* Hooke's law, 21.

ELASTICITY

When forces act on an object that cannot move, they may change its size or shape. Some substances, like rubber, return to their original form when the force is removed. These are called **elastic** substances.

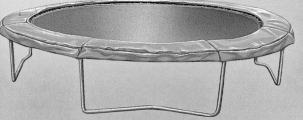

A trampoline is elastic. When the forces stretching it are removed, it goes back to its original shape.

The amount that an elastic substance will stretch obeys Hooke's law*, which states that if the force increases in equal steps, so does the stretch.

If something is stretched beyond its elastic limit, though, Hooke's law no longer works. The **elastic limit** is the point at which a substance alters permanently when it is stretched.

A rubber band is elastic, but will snap if you stretch it too far (that is, beyond its elastic limit).

Some materials do not return to their original form after being stretched and they can hold a new shape. This is called **plastic** behaviour.

Modelling clay behaves in a plastic way.

After it has been modelled, the clay keeps the shape that it has been given. This is an example of plastic behaviour.

Internet links

Go to **www.usborne-quicklinks.com** for links to the following websites:

Website 1 Take part in an interactive demonstration of moments of force.

Website 2 See how the lever and fulcrum work as you investigate an interactive experiment.

Website 3 Explore the physics of tennis with an online activity and discover how different forces affect a tennis ball.

Website 4 Find out more about elasticity and earthquakes and watch a simple animation about the elastic limit of a fence.

DYNAMICS

The study of how forces affect movement is called **dynamics**. The terms inertia and momentum are used to describe how easily objects both start and stop moving. There are three laws of motion which explain the principles governing the movement of all objects. These laws were formulated by the English scientist, Isaac Newton, in 1687.

Isaac Newton, English scientist (1642-1727)

NEWTON'S LAWS OF MOTION

Isaac Newton made important discoveries about many subjects, including motion, gravity and light. His three **laws of motion** have had a major influence on scientific thinking.

Newton's first law states that if an object is not being acted on by a force, it will either stay still or continue moving at a constant speed in a straight line. This is the principle of inertia (see right).

Newton's second law states that any force acting on an object will change its motion. How much change there is depends on the object's mass and the size of the resultant force.

Newton's third law states that when a force acts on an object, the object exerts an equal force in the opposite direction. The first force is called the **action** and the second is the **reaction**.

To start this truck moving, it will take a force to overcome its inertia. (See Newton's first law.)

The same force of wind will move a pine cone less than a leaf because the cone's mass is greater. (See Newton's second law.)

The ball exerts a force on a bat, felt as the slowing down of the bat, that is equal and opposite to the force the bat exerts on the ball. (See Newton's third law.)

INERTIA

Objects resist change in their movement. This tendency, called **inertia**, applies to stationary and moving objects. The inertia of a stationary object makes it hard to get moving. If moving, inertia makes the object want to continue moving in a straight line. It takes a force to overcome inertia.

Without the restraining force of a seatbelt or airbag, the inertia of this crash test dummy would send it through the windscreen.

The larger an object's mass, the more inertia it has. A big animal has to exert more force to change its movement than a small one. Twice the mass means twice the inertia.

This adult elephant has five times as much mass as the baby. Its inertia is five times as great.

MOMENTUM

Momentum is a measure of an object's tendency to carry on moving. It is found by multiplying the object's mass by its velocity. The greater the mass and the velocity, the greater the momentum. Like velocity, momentum is a vector quantity, which means it has both size and direction.

Buzzard

Seagull

If a buzzard and seagull are flying at the same speed, the bird with the greater mass (the buzzard) has greater momentum.

This full trolley's mass is 10kg and its velocity is 1m/s east. Its momentum is 10kg m/s east.

This almost empty trolley has a mass of 2kg and a velocity of 5m/s east. Its momentum is also 10kg m/s east.

An object with a small mass can have the same momentum as an object with a large mass, providing it is moving faster.

See for yourself

Contraptions called Newton's cradles are sometimes sold as interesting, grown-up "toys" which show conservation of momentum. See if you can find one. As the first ball hits the other balls, its momentum is transferred through to the last ball, making it move.

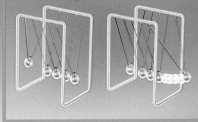

CONSERVATION OF MOMENTUM

When two objects collide, such as the pink ball and the blue ball shown here, their total momentum stays the same as it was just before the collision. This is called the **law of conservation of momentum**. So when one object loses momentum in a collision, the other gains the same amount.

The pink ball rolls towards the blue ball.

As the pink ball hits the blue ball, it transfers momentum through the blue ball to the red ball.

As their masses are the same, the red ball accelerates to the speed that the pink ball had before the collision.

Internet links

Go to **www.usborne-quicklinks.com** for links to the following websites:

Website 1 Find lots of science in a game of baseball.

Website 2 Try a marbles experiment to see how momentum is passed on.

Website 3 Browse a library of biographies of famous scientists, including Newton and Pascal.

Website 4 Investigate momentum with an interactive 'Newton's Cradle'.

Website 5 An illustrated explanation of Newton's three laws of motion.

FRICTION

When a moving object is touching another object, like a coin sliding across a table, the moving object slows down. The force that causes this is called **friction**. The rougher the surfaces are, and the harder they press together, the more friction there will be. Friction occurs in liquids and gases as well as between solids. Anything that experiences friction warms up.

New shoe

Old shoe

Constant friction with the floor means a ballet dancer's shoes wear out after a few weeks.

USING FRICTION

Friction is useful in some situations and a nuisance in others. If there were no friction between surfaces, it would be impossible to grip anything.

Many kinds of machines make use of friction. With too little friction between tyres and the surface of a road, for example, drivers wouldn't be able to stop their vehicles from sliding around.

The skis' smooth undersides minimize friction with the snow, allowing them to slide very easily. However, their sharp edges create friction when the skier turns, enabling him to control his speed and direction.

Water and mud on the road reduce friction because they act as lubricants (see opposite page). The grooves on a tyre channel water or mud through them, so that the raised rubber pieces (the **tread**) can grip the surface of the road.

Some devices need friction to be able to work at all. For example, friction between a match and a matchbox generates enough heat for chemicals in the match head to burn. All brakes work by using friction to slow down a vehicle's wheels.

Disc brake

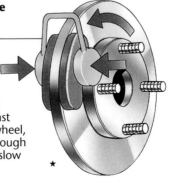

Brake pad

Brake pads press against this steel wheel, causing enough friction to slow it down.

The soles of sports shoes are made from materials, such as rubber, which provide a lot of friction.

REDUCING FRICTION

Lots of friction between machine parts is damaging. It causes wear and tear, and some of the energy needed to run the machine is wasted on heat instead of movement. Oil is used to reduce friction because it is smoother than any solid surface, so it allows objects to slide across each other more easily. A liquid used like this is called a **lubricant**.

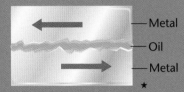

Metal
Oil
Metal

Magnification shows how a smooth-seeming metal surface is actually fairly rough. A layer of oil between moving metal surfaces reduces friction.

A layer of **ball bearings** between two surfaces in a machine reduces the amount of contact between the surfaces. This reduces the friction between them, and the amount of wear.

Ball bearings lie around the axle of this wheel. They rotate as the wheel turns.

FRICTION IN AIR AND SPACE

Drag, or **air resistance**, is the friction that occurs between air and any object moving through it (see also page 44). In space, there is no air, so there is no friction. The Space Shuttle, for instance, experiences no friction as it moves through space, until it re-enters the Earth's atmosphere.

Drag slows down the Shuttle as it enters the Earth's atmosphere. The friction between the Shuttle and the air makes it glow red hot.

See for yourself

You can see how ball bearings reduce friction using some marbles and a big book. First, push the book along on its own. Notice the friction. Now put marbles under the book and push again. The marbles roll between the book and the surface, reducing friction.

Marble

STREAMLINING

To reduce drag, vehicles are designed so that they are **streamlined**. Streamlining lets the air flow over a vehicle in smooth lines, so that it can move forwards with less effort.

Car manufacturers use jets of smoke to test the streamlining of new cars. Here, the Ford Ka is being tested.

FRICTION IN WATER

Water is denser* than air, so more friction acts on objects moving through water. Fish, and sea mammals such as whales, have naturally streamlined bodies that reduce the friction between themselves and the water.

Water flows easily over a whale's streamlined body.

Internet links

Go to **www.usborne-quicklinks.com** for links to the following websites:

Websites 1-2 Find out more about friction and discover the scientific principles behind cycling and ice hockey.

Website 3 Play an entertaining game to find out the effect of air friction on your body. Get it wrong and disaster will follow.

Website 4 Discover more about friction in everyday life then record how friction affects you.

Website 5 An online friction experiment using wind-up toys.

Website 6 Record your results online as you carry out a fun, interactive experiment about friction and forces.

* Density, 40.

MOTION

In physics, **motion** is the study of how something moves, whether it is a planet moving around the Sun or a snowboarder flying through the air. An object's motion is usually described in terms of its velocity and acceleration, and its motion only changes if a force, or several forces, act on it.

Snowboarders can reach speeds of 22m/s, which is the same as 80km/h.

SPEED

Speed is a measure of how fast an object is moving. The average speed of a moving object can be calculated by dividing the distance it has travelled by the time it has taken to do so.

Speed calculation

This cyclist has gone 500m in 40 seconds. The calculation below gives her average speed.

$$\text{Average speed} = \frac{\text{Distance (metres)}}{\text{Time (seconds)}}$$

$$= \frac{500}{40} = 12.5\text{m/s}$$

Speed is a scalar quantity. This means that it measures the amount of speed a moving object has, but not the direction in which it is moving. In physics, the unit of measurement most often used is metres per second (m/s). However, you will often see kilometres per hour (km/h) as well. This measures how far something will go in an hour.

CHANGING SPEED

The speed of a moving object can change from moment to moment. A sprinter, for instance, runs slowest when setting off at the start of a race. He is likely to be running fastest as he approaches the finishing line. The speed of something at any particular moment is called its **instantaneous speed**.

For example, in 1999 the men's world record for the 100m race was 9.84 seconds. This is an average speed of 10.16m/s. After running 1m of the race, though, the winner's instantaneous speed might have been 3m/s. After a few more metres, it could have been as high as 11m/s.

Sprinters during a race

VELOCITY

Velocity measures the direction in which an object is travelling as well as its speed. This makes velocity a vector quantity. The velocity of a moving object can change even if its speed remains exactly the same because a change in direction changes the velocity.

Although this car is travelling at a steady speed of 10km/h, its velocity is changing all the time because it is constantly changing direction.

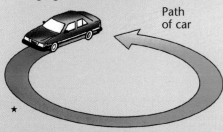

Path of car

Velocity is measured in metres per second (m/s) in a particular direction. For instance, someone walking north at 1.5m/s has a velocity of 1.5m/s north. **Relative velocity** is the velocity a moving object appears to have when viewed from another moving object.

These stunt jets are both flying at a velocity of 83m/s in the same direction.

The velocity of one jet relative to the other (from the point of view of either) is zero.

ACCELERATION

Acceleration is a change in the velocity of an object, that is, a change in its speed or direction in a given time. In physics, acceleration is measured in metres per second per second, or m/s^2. This is not as confusing as it looks. If something accelerates at $1m/s^2$ (1 metre per second per second), it gets faster by one metre a second, every second.

A decrease in velocity is called **negative acceleration**, or **deceleration**. Any change in speed or direction means that an object accelerates, or decelerates, as both affect velocity. Car manufacturers usually consider acceleration in kilometres (or miles) per hour per second. This is simply using different units to measure the same thing.

If a car is travelling at a steady 50km/h in one direction, its acceleration is zero. This is because neither its speed nor its direction are changing.

This Porsche 911 Turbo accelerates from 0-100km/h in 4.5 seconds. This works out at an average acceleration of $6.2m/s^2$.

When they first leave the plane, the Earth's gravity causes skydivers to accelerate at a rate of $9.8m/s^2$.

When skydivers open their parachutes, they suddenly decelerate.

See for yourself

Make three small balls using modelling clay. Drop each one from a different height. The greater the drop, the bigger the dent in the ball when it hits the floor. This is because the further things fall, the faster they go.

The ball on the left falls furthest, so it is most squashed when it lands.

Internet links

Go to **www.usborne-quicklinks.com** for links to the following websites:

Website 1 Lots of practical information about speed.

Website 2 Try an interactive game where you have to pick a 'winner' in a race about motion.

Website 3 Race vehicles in an online speed and acceleration experiment.

Website 4 Try an online quiz on definitions of motion and energy.

Website 5 Helpful explanations of velocity and acceleration, with examples.

TERMINAL VELOCITY

When something falls through a gas or liquid it accelerates, at a decreasing rate, until it reaches its maximum constant velocity. This is called its **terminal velocity**.

As an example, imagine skydivers jumping from a plane. They start to accelerate the moment they jump from the plane.

They continue accelerating, but at a slower and slower rate, until they reach a speed of about 200km/h. At this point they stop accelerating.

When the acceleration has dropped to zero, they have reached their terminal velocity.

When something begins to fall, it accelerates quickly.

The longer it falls, the less quickly it accelerates.

When it stops accelerating. It has reached its terminal velocity.

RESISTANCE

The pull of **gravity** is the force that makes an object accelerate downwards. But as the object starts to move, it experiences **resistance**, an upward force, from the gas or liquid it is falling through. The faster the object falls, the stronger the resistance becomes, until it equals the downward force of the weight of the object. The object stops accelerating at this point and has reached its terminal velocity.

The terminal velocity of an object is slower in a liquid than it is in a gas. This is because a liquid provides more resistance than a gas. As a result, the forces become balanced earlier and the object stops accelerating sooner.

A falling coin takes longer to reach its terminal velocity in air than in water.

MOTION IN A CIRCLE

All moving objects try to travel in a straight line (see Newton's first law, page 24). The force which makes something turn in a circle instead is called a **centripetal force**. This is any force that constantly pulls towards the centre of a circle.

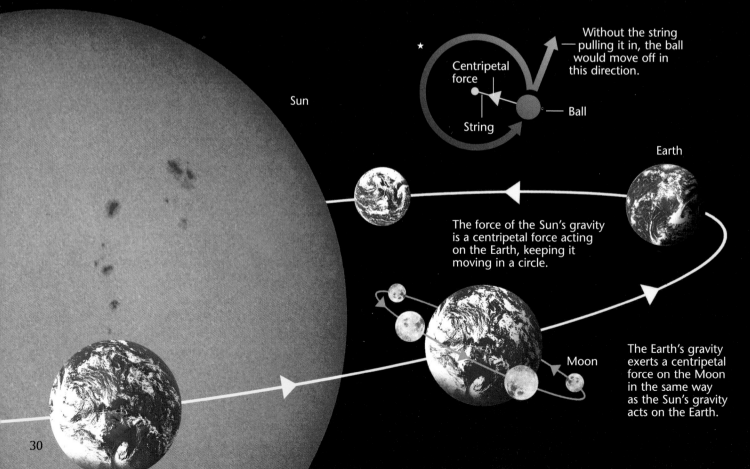

Without the string pulling it in, the ball would move off in this direction.

Centripetal force

String

Ball

Sun

Earth

The force of the Sun's gravity is a centripetal force acting on the Earth, keeping it moving in a circle.

Moon

The Earth's gravity exerts a centripetal force on the Moon in the same way as the Sun's gravity acts on the Earth.

CENTRIPETAL FORCE - AN EXAMPLE

If you tie a small object to a piece of string and whirl it around your head, the pull of the string on the object is a centripetal force. As long as you whirl fast enough, the object will not fall in on you. If you let go of the string, you remove the centripetal force and the object will fly off at a tangent, as when an athlete throws the "hammer".

1. The athlete pulls on the wire to make the hammer move.

2. His pull is a centripetal force on the hammer as it moves.

3. The faster the hammer moves, the more centripetal force is needed.

4. The hammer flies off when the centripetal force is removed.

GYROSCOPES

Gyroscopes are wheels that can spin very fast within a frame. The centripetal force created means that the frame can resist the force of gravity. It can even tilt steeply without toppling over. However, when the wheel slows, the gyroscope will fall. (You can buy gyroscopes in some toy shops.)

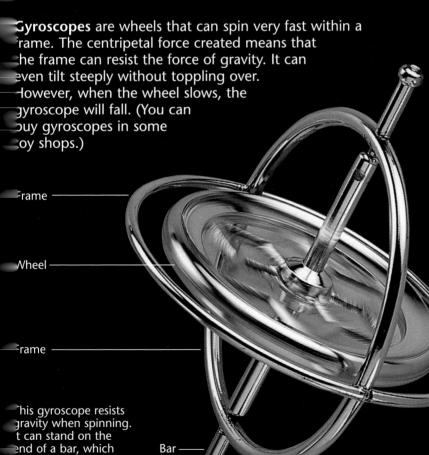

Frame —————

Wheel —————

Frame —————

Bar ———

This gyroscope resists gravity when spinning. It can stand on the end of a bar, which is attached to the frame directly beneath the middle of the spinning wheel.

See for yourself

You can see the effect of centripetal force for yourself.

Put a marble in a plastic bowl and move the bowl so that the marble moves in a circle. You have created a centripetal force on the marble.

However, the marble will fly out of the bowl when it reaches a certain speed. The centripetal force is not strong enough to keep it moving in such a tight circle.

Notice that the marble flies off in a straight line.

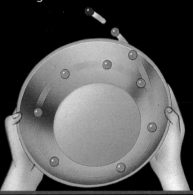

Internet links

Go to **www.usborne-quicklinks.com** for links to the following websites:

Website 1 Useful online lesson on the physics of motion and the words used to describe the way things move.

Website 2 See how different speeds and angles affect the orbit of a comet.

Website 3 Learn more about the physics of bicycle wheels.

Website 4 Control the different forces to see if you can get the cannon ball to hit the target.

Website 5 Learn about the history, inventors and the future of rollercoasters and explore an interactive physics diagram.

Website 6 Experiment with centripetal force with an interactive model of a carousel.

Web site 7 A simple experiment that shows how centripetal force works.

GRAVITY

The force of **gravity** attracts objects to each other. This attraction is not noticeable unless one of the objects is very large, such as a planet. The area within which gravity has an effect is called a **gravitational field**. The Earth and Moon both have gravitational fields, although the Earth's is a lot stronger than the Moon's because it is a much bigger object.

The force of the Sun's gravity keeps a belt of rocks, called asteroids, orbiting around it.

GRAVITY AND MASS

The strength of the pull of gravity between two objects depends on how far apart they are and their masses. **Mass** is the amount of matter that an object contains and this never varies. Any two objects, such as two tomatoes, are attracted to each other, but as their masses are small, the force of gravity between them is tiny and there is no visible effect.

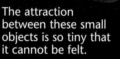

The attraction between these small objects is so tiny that it cannot be felt.

EARTH'S GRAVITY

The force of gravity between the Earth and anything on it is extremely noticeable because the mass of the Earth is so large.

The pull of the Earth's gravity makes any object, such as this conker, fall to the ground.

GRAVITY AND WEIGHT

Weight is a measure of the pull of gravity on an object's mass. The further away an object is from the centre of the Earth, the less the pull of gravity on it. Because of this, you weigh slightly less at a high altitude (for example, at the top of a high mountain) than at the bottom, even though your mass stays the same.

When they are space walking, astronauts weigh far less than they do on Earth. They are so far from the Earth's centre that the planet's gravity has little effect on them.

CENTRE OF GRAVITY

Gravity affects every part of an object, but there is one point where the object's whole weight seems to act. This is its **centre of gravity**. An object can often be balanced at its centre of gravity.

X = centre of gravity

Regularly shaped and symmetrical objects, like this handweight, have their centre of gravity exactly in the middle.

A **stable object** returns to its original position when tilted. Centre of gravity is the key to stability. If an object tilts, but its centre of gravity remains above its base, it won't fall over.

A racing car is very stable. Its centre of gravity is low and its base is wide.

An **unstable object** has its centre of gravity high up, and has a relatively narrow base. If an unstable object is tilted, its centre of gravity soon stops being above its base.

A stationary motorbike is a good example of an unstable object. It will soon fall over when it is tilted.

Tall, narrow things aren't necessarily unstable. For example, a double-decker bus is built so that its centre of gravity is low, making it stable.

The bottom part of the bus is heavy, containing the engine, wheels and chassis. The top part of the bus is light. As a result, the centre of gravity is low.

See for yourself

Follow these steps to find the centre of gravity of a piece of paper.

1. Hold up the paper and let it dangle.

2. Hold it against a wall and draw a line straight down the paper from where you are holding it.

3. Hold the paper at a different point and repeat step 2. The centre of gravity will be where the lines cross. If you carry on repeating this, the lines should cross in the same place.

Stable object   **X** = centre of gravity

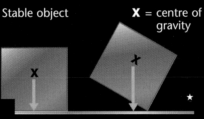

X

Unless a stable object is tilted a very long way, its centre of gravity stays above its base. As a result, it tends to fall back onto its base.

Unstable object   **X** = centre of gravity

When an unstable object is tilted, its centre of gravity quickly stops being above its base. This causes the object to topple over.

Tall, stable object   **X** = centre of gravity

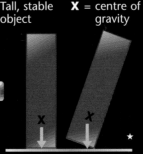

With a low centre of gravity, the tall object must tilt a long way before it topples.

EARTH AND MOON

As the Moon goes around the Earth, its gravity pulls at the planet. This has an effect on the seas of the Earth, which rise and fall. Areas where the water has risen are having a **high tide**. Areas that are not having a high tide are having a **low tide**.

The Moon's effect on the tides

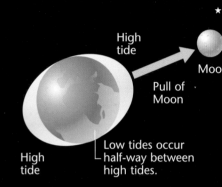

High tide

Moon

Pull of Moon

High tide

Low tides occur half-way between high tides.

Similarly, the Earth's gravity also pulls at the Moon. It is providing the force, called centripetal force, which is needed to keep the Moon locked in orbit around the Earth itself.

For more information on centripetal force, see *Motion in a Circle*, on page 30.

Internet links

Go to **www.usborne-quicklinks.com** for links to the following websites:

Website 1 What would happen if gravity was switched off? Try a 'thought experiment' in a fun guide to gravity.

Website 2 Check your weight on any of the nine planets, and find out why it differs.

Website 3 Short animated tutorial about mass, weight and gravity.

Website 4 Explore gravity by playing a lunar lander game. The try landing on Earth and Jupiter to see how gravity differs there.

Website 5 Useful online lesson on gravity.

PRESSURE

A needle will go through a piece of cloth, but with the same amount of force, a pencil will not. The differently shaped points of the needle and pencil exert different amounts of pressure. Pressure is everywhere. It operates many machines and affects our weather. Solids, liquids and gases all apply pressure to the surfaces they touch.

Sharp scissors cut well because the blades exert pressure over a tiny area.

WHAT IS PRESSURE?

When a force acts on an object it exerts **pressure**. The pressure acts at a right-angle to the object itself, and its strength depends on the amount of force and the area over which it is applied. For example, someone walking on soft snow will sink into it in normal shoes but not if they wear snowshoes. The person's weight is the same but snowshoes spread the weight over a larger area. This reduces the pressure.

The bottom of a snowshoe is about six times bigger than the sole of a foot.

ATMOSPHERIC PRESSURE

Atmospheric pressure is the weight of air pressing down on the Earth's surface. Over one square metre, the weight of air pressing down is heavier than a large elephant. Air pressure is greatest near the ground, and reduces with height. At 10,000m above the ground, where jets fly, air pressure is very low as there is less air pressing down on anything up there. Less air means less oxygen, and aircraft have pressurized cabins so that people can breathe. The air pressure inside the plane is kept roughly the same as it would be at ground level.

Pressure is measured in **pascals (Pa)**, which are named after the French scientist Blaise Pascal (1623-1662), who made many discoveries about air pressure.

CHANGING WEATHER

Atmospheric pressure is measured in **millibars (mb)**. Weather changes as the pressure changes, with low pressure signalling bad weather and high pressure bringing a settled, fine spell. For example, usual atmospheric pressure at sea level is 1,013mb. However, this can fall to 910mb in a hurricane.

Heavy rains and strong winds are brought by low atmospheric pressure.

PRESSURE IN FLUIDS

Fluids (liquids and gases) change shape according to the container that they are in. The pressure inside them acts outwards in all directions.

Air inside a beach ball pushes out in all directions, keeping it blown up. ★

Liquid in a glass exerts pressure against the sides as well as the bottom. ★

HYDRAULIC MACHINES

Hydraulic machines are machines powered by liquid pressure. A liquid cannot be squashed, so if you press one part of the liquid, pressure increases throughout and the liquid has to move somewhere.

This robot arm works using hydraulic pressure.

Car brakes are hydraulic. Brake fluid is pushed through the brake system, forcing the wheels to slow down.

How a car's footbrake works

Driver presses pedal, pushing piston (1) which forces fluid through cylinder (2). Fluid goes down pipe into two more cylinders (red arrows). These press brake pads (3) against disc in wheel. Friction* slows down wheel (4).

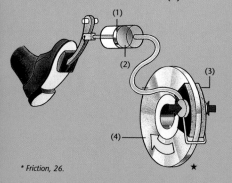

(1)
(2)
(3)
(4)

Friction, 26. ★

PNEUMATIC MACHINES

Pneumatic machines are driven by the pressure of gases, usually air. Unlike liquid, air can be compressed into a smaller space, and this increases its pressure.

A pneumatic drill, for example, is powered by a piston which squashes air inside the drill to a very high pressure. The compressed air pushes out with enough force to power the drill to crack rock.

Pneumatic drill

A foam and water fire extinguisher is a pneumatic machine which uses compressed carbon dioxide gas.

How a fire extinguisher works

Squeezing handle (1) releases carbon dioxide gas from canister (2). Gas pushes down on a mixture of water and detergent (3), forcing it up a tube (4) and through a hose (5). It shoots out as a jet of foam and water.

(1)
(2)
(3)
(4)
(5)
★

See for yourself

This experiment shows how air pushes out in all directions. You need a lightweight book and a plastic bag.

Put the book on the bag and blow into the bag.

Air pressure increases inside the bag and lifts the book.

Internet links

Go to **www.usborne-quicklinks.com** for links to the following websites:

Website 1 Find out about the effect that pressure has on underwater divers.

Website 2 Find out how a soap dispenser works then explore more about pneumatic systems and machines.

Website 3 Try a simple but effective pressure experiment at home.

Website 4 Learn about pressure and try some simple tests to see the difference between force and pressure.

Website 5 Simple explanations of pressure in a gas or a liquid.

SIMPLE MACHINES

All machines make physical work easier to do by taking the effort needed to operate them and using it in a more efficient way. Simple machines are devices such as levers and screws. Complex machines, such as drills and cranes, are made up of combinations of simple machines.

The wheel, one of the most important devices ever invented, forms the basis of many machines.

OVERCOMING LOAD

To move any object, you need to overcome a force called the **load**, which is often the weight of the object. A simple machine helps you to do this by taking the force of your **effort** and applying it more efficiently.

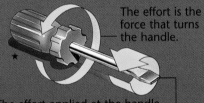

The effort is the force that turns the handle.

The effort applied at the handle creates a greater force here, enabling the screwdriver to overcome the load applied by the screw.

It is possible to find out how much more force a simple machine provides compared with the amount of effort that is put in. This is done by dividing the load by the amount of effort used, and is called the **force ratio**.

The load exerted by the nutshell is 4N. But squeezing the nutcracker handles to crack it only takes 1N. So the force ratio is 4:1.

If a force ratio is 4:1, the load which the machine overcomes is four times greater than the effort used. Machines like this are called **force magnifiers**.

LEVERS

A **lever** is a rod that turns at a fixed point, called a **fulcrum**, making it easier to perform a task. There are three classes of lever, each with a different arrangement of the fulcrum, effort and load.

A **class one lever** has the fulcrum between the effort and the load.

Fulcrum

Effort

Load

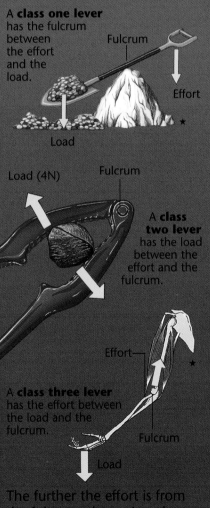

Load (4N)

Fulcrum

A **class two lever** has the load between the effort and the fulcrum.

Effort (1N)

Effort

A **class three lever** has the effort between the load and the fulcrum.

Fulcrum

Load

The further the effort is from the fulcrum, the easier a lever is to use, so longer levers are generally more useful. (See *Turning Forces* on page 23.)

WHEELS

When a **wheel** turns a rod (such as a steering wheel turning a steering column in a car) the force applied on the wheel is turned into a bigger force by the rod. The bigger the wheel is, the more easily the rod turns.

Turning the steering wheel exerts a big enough force at the steering column to turn a car's front wheels.

Steering column

When an axle is turned, a wheel connected to it will convert the axle's circular motion into a straight line motion that can move loads across the ground. A car's wheels are an example of this. The wheel turns further than the axle because it is bigger.

See for yourself

To see how a class one lever works, put a pencil under the middle of a rigid ruler. Put a lightweight book on one end.

Ruler   Press down
Book   to raise book.

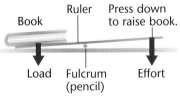

Load   Fulcrum   Effort
        (pencil)

Try changing the position of the pencil under the ruler. The further the effort is from the fulcrum, the easier it is to lift the load.

PULLEYS

Pulleys help to lift heavy loads and are often used in lifts and cranes. The load is attached to a rope which passes around one or more grooved wheels. When the other end of the rope is pulled, the load is lifted.

Pulley

Pulleys let you pull down instead of up, so you can use your weight to help.

The more wheels a pulley has, the easier it is to lift a load, as the weight of the load is spread out over more rope.

This crane works like a giant pulley. The rope is made of strong steel cable. The pulling strength is provided by the crane's engine.

The strong steel cable passes over grooved wheels.

The cable can lift very heavy objects, such as steel and concrete building materials.

SCREWS

A **screw** has an axle and a thread which work together like an inclined plane (see below) wrapped around a cylinder. The axle is the cylinder and the thread the inclined plane.

The turning screw converts the force applied into a much greater straight line force. As a result, the axle easily drives straight into the object.

A corkscrew converts a turning motion into a straight line force.

GEARS

Gears are used to change speed in many different kinds of complex machines, from cars to clocks. They do this by changing the size of a turning force.

Gears consist of two or more toothed wheels, or **cogs**, that fit into each other, so that turning one cog turns the other. A large cog makes a smaller one turn faster.

This gear changes the size and direction of the turning force.

This clock works using a complicated system of geared wheels.

The crane's engine is housed here.

Internet links

Go to **www.usborne-quicklinks.com** for links to the following websites:

Website 1 Find out why bikes are such an efficient form of transport.

Website 2 Raise an obelisk using a simple machine.

Website 3 Read about Leonardo da Vinci and machines he invented.

Website 4 Interactive games about simple machines found around your home.

Websites 5-6 Online activities and investigations about simple machines.

Website 7 Machines in history.

INCLINED PLANES

An **inclined plane** is just a slope, like a ramp. It is easier to move an object up an inclined plane than vertically upwards, because you travel further, so less force is needed for the same amount of work.

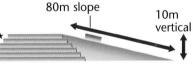

80m slope

10m vertical

If you push an object eight times as far up an inclined plane as lifting it straight up, you only need one eighth of the force.

USING SIMPLE MACHINES

Simple machines can be used to make up more complex machines. Here are some examples. Even animals, such as the lobster on the right, can have body parts which work in the same way as a machine.

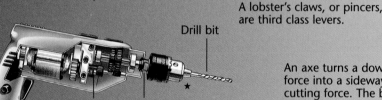

Big gear wheel

Small gear wheel

Handle

Blades

Gears on a whisk increase the size of the turning force needed to move the handle, so that the blades can be turned very fast.

Propellers are a simple form of screw. They are used to push ships through water – and to pull aircraft through the air.

Archimedes' screw was an early device for pumping water from rivers or lakes.

Handle

Water was drawn up on the inclined planes of a turning screw.

Drill bit

Gears   Drive shaft

An electric drill combines gears and a screw at the tip, called a **bit**. The gears change the speed at which the bit rotates, so that it can drill a hole quickly or slowly.

A lobster's claws, or pincers, are third class levers.

Fulcrum

An axe turns a downward force into a sideways cutting force. The blade is a **wedge** that pushes apart as it cuts down.

Your front teeth, called incisors, are wedges. They work like axes, pushing food apart as they cut down.

Downward force

Sideways force

A motor provides power to a system of gears and wheels which move the stairs and handrails on an escalator.

Scissors are class one levers. The blades are sharp wedges that force surfaces apart.

Fulcrum

A fan is a third class lever. When you wave it, your wrist acts as the fulcrum.

The Ancient Egyptians, who built the pyramids, may have used inclined planes, in the form of spiral slopes, to push enormous blocks of stone up into place. The tallest pyramids were about 146m high.

WORK AND POWER

I n science, the word "work" has a particular meaning. **Work** is done when a force makes an object move. Work is only done when the object moves.

MEASURING WORK

Work transfers energy from one object to another and, like energy, is measured in **joules (J)**. One joule equals the work done (and energy transferred) when a force of 1 newton (N) moves an object 1 metre in the direction of the force.

If this man pushes the box with a force of 100 newtons for 3 metres, he performs 300 joules of work.

POWER

Power is the rate at which work is done, or energy is transferred. It is measured in **watts (W)**, named after James Watt, and is worked out by dividing the work done by the time taken to do it.

It takes twice as much power to move the box 3 metres in one minute as to move it 3 metres in two minutes.

AN EXAMPLE OF WORK

In the picture, the male dancer's lifting force is overcoming the force of gravity, and work is being done as he raises the ballerina in the air.

The male dancer is using his energy to lift the ballerina. Most of this energy is being converted to potential energy* in the dancer in the air. Also, some heat energy is being released by the male dancer's body.

The ballerina has to do work as she moves her body into the correct pose.

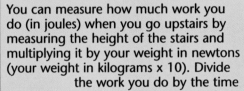

You can measure how much work you do (in joules) when you go upstairs by measuring the height of the stairs and multiplying it by your weight in newtons (your weight in kilograms x 10). Divide the work you do by the time it takes to do it to find out how much power you exert (in watts). The quicker you go, the more power you exert.

Height of stairs

Internet links

Website 1

Website 2 Find out how much work your body

Website 3 Read a short biography of James Watt

Website 4 Read an explanation of joules, power and watts

* Potential energy, 8.

FLOATING

Why do some substances float in water, but not others? And why are there so few substances that are able to float in air? By understanding the principles of floating (and sinking), engineers can build ships out of metals that are heavier than the water they float in, and design airships and hot-air balloons that can float in the air.

WHY THINGS FLOAT

When an object is put into water, it pushes aside, or **displaces**, some of the water. It takes up the space where the water was, and the level of the water rises.

According to legend, the Ancient Greek scientist Archimedes (287-212BC) first realized how objects displace water when he got into his bath.

This is a medieval picture of Archimedes making his discovery.

Water pushes back against an object placed in it with a force called **upthrust**. If this is the same as the weight of the object, the object floats. The weight of the object and the weight of the water it displaces are equal.

Hot-air balloons are filled with air that is lighter than the cool air outside them. They rise up because hot air floats.

ARCHIMEDES' PRINCIPLE

Archimedes' principle states that the upthrust acting on an object is equal to the weight of the fluid that the object displaces. An object will sink into a fluid, such as water, and keep on sinking unless the force of the upthrust from the fluid becomes equal to the weight of the object.

Water is displaced (yellow arrows) as boat is lowered. Upthrust (red arrow) pushes back on boat.

When upthrust of water equals weight of boat, boat settles on water and floats steadily.

DENSITY

One object may float while another of the same size may sink. Same-sized objects have different weights if their density is different. **Density** is a measure of the amount of matter in an object (its **mass**) compared to its volume (size).

A steel ball is heavier than an apple of the same size because it is denser. Its matter is packed more tightly together. The apple floats (just) in water but the steel ball sinks.

FLOATING IN THE AIR

Air, like water, pushes back at an object with a force called upthrust. This equals the weight of air pushed aside by the object. If the upthrust equals the weight of the object, the object floats. But air is so light that few things float in it. Hot-air balloons and helium-filled airships can both float in air, though, because hot air and helium are both lighter than cold air.

Airships are built so that the helium is held in a series of separate cells. If one cell bursts, only the helium in that section will be lost.

This cutaway drawing shows an airship filled with helium gas, which is lighter than air.

Helium gas cell

Metal frames give the airship a stable shape.

HOW SHIPS FLOAT

Modern ships are made of steel, which is eight times denser than water. But they don't sink because their overall density is lower than water. This is because ships are hollow. All the space inside them makes them less dense than water. Their huge volume pushes aside (or displaces) a large amount of water and so creates a lot of upthrust on the ship.

Even when fully laden, a container ship still displaces so much water that it floats. The displaced water creates a massive upthrust on the huge ship.

RELATIVE DENSITIES

For an object to float in water, its density needs to be less than, or the same as, the density of water. If not, the water cannot provide enough upthrust to support it.

The **relative density** of an object is its density when compared to the density of water. The relative density of water is 1, so an object will sink if its relative density is more than 1, but float if it is 1 or less.

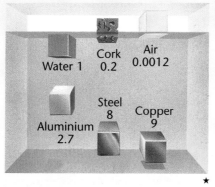

This picture shows the relative densities of different substances. Nearly all metals are denser than water.

Water 1   Cork 0.2   Air 0.0012
Aluminium 2.7   Steel 8   Copper 9

See for yourself

You can use a ball of modelling clay to show how a ship floats. If you drop the ball into water it will sink. This is because the ball is denser than the water. If you shape the same piece of clay into a hollow bowl, though, it should float.

Although it is the same weight as the ball, the bowl floats because it pushes aside more water. The force of the upthrust equals its weight.

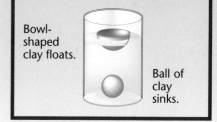

Bowl-shaped clay floats.

Ball of clay sinks.

Internet links

Go to **www.usborne-quicklinks.com** for links to the following websites:

Website 1 Find out about gases, density and buoyancy. Includes pictures and videos.

Website 2 See the specifications of the Breitling Orbiter, the first hot-air balloon to circle the Earth non-stop, on this easy to use site.

Website 3 Learn about buoyancy, with an experiment and links to more activities.

Website 4 Floating facts and mini-quiz.

Web site 5 The history and science of ballooning, and a virtual flight.

SHIPS AND BOATS

Ships and boats once relied on the wind or human strength for their power. The invention of engines meant that propellers* could be used to drive ships through the water. More recent boat designs include hydrofoils and hovercraft.

Viking ship

In the ninth century, the Vikings used ships like this. For power, they used sails as well as oars.

Tankers

Tankers carry oil or other liquid cargo in tanks. Big tankers, called supertankers, are the largest ships in the world.

Helicopter landing pad

Control deck

Hovercraft

A hovercraft (also called an Air-Cushion Vehicle, or ACV) skims over the water on a cushion of air inside a rubber skirt.

Rudders
Fins
Engines
Propellers drive the hovercraft forward.
Control cabin
Cutaway view of rubber skirt

Cruise ships

Large, luxurious cruise ships are designed to carry hundreds of people on holidays.

Hydrofoils

Hydrofoils have stilts attached to underwater "wings" called foils. When a hydrofoil speeds up, its hull lifts out of the water, reducing water resistance. Two designs of foil are surface-piercing foils and ladder foils.

Hull
Surface-piercing foil

Hydrofoil with surface-piercing foils

Hydrofoil with ladder foils

Container ships

Container ships carry goods in large metal boxes. These can be unloaded or loaded quickly by cranes. One ship can carry hundreds of containers.

Containers

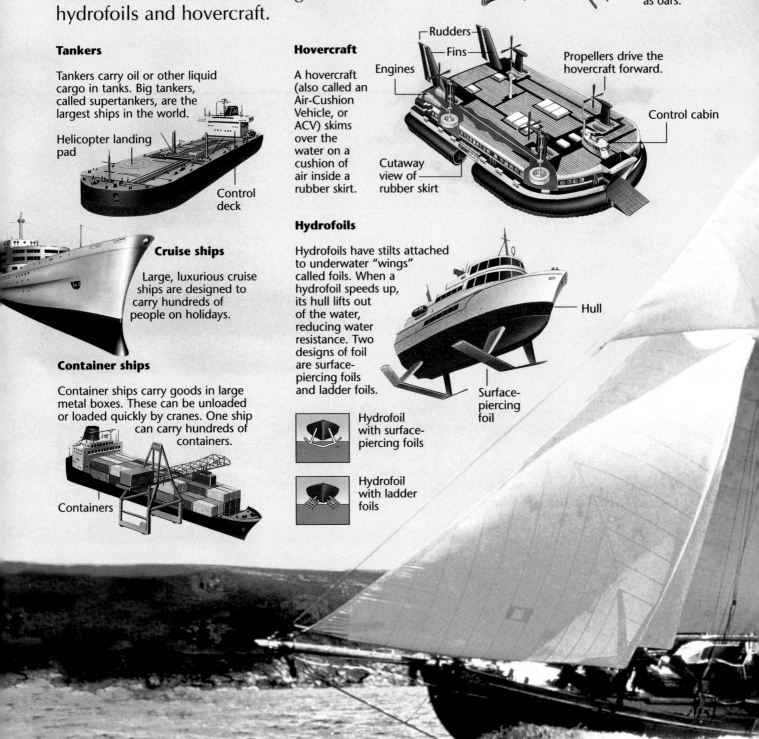

* Propellers, 38.

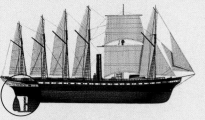

Iron ship

This nineteenth century boat had sails and a steam engine that drove a propeller (shown with the rudder in the circle). It had an iron hull.

Clipper

Clippers were used in the nineteenth century to carry goods around the world. They had so many sails that they could reach speeds of nearly 40km/h.

SUBMARINES

Submarines can dive and surface by altering their relative density*. They carry large containers called **ballast tanks**. When air is expelled from these tanks and replaced with water, the submarine's density increases and it dives. When it needs to surface, air is pumped back into the tanks and water is forced back out. This makes the submarine less dense, and it rises to the surface.

The ballast tanks are placed between the submarine's two hulls.

Periscope

A submarine dives as its ballast tanks are filled with water.

Outer hull

A submarine rises as air is pumped back into the tanks and water is forced out.

Inner hull

Submarines have powerful propellers to drive them through the water. Some have engines driven by nuclear power.

Propeller

Racing yacht

This old racing yacht was built using heavy wood, and has weighty canvas sails. Modern versions use more lightweight materials, so they are faster and easier to steer.

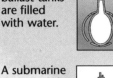

See for yourself

Put the top on an empty plastic bottle and hold it under water. Let it go and the bottle will shoot up to the surface.

Now fill the bottle with water. You are making the bottle denser, so it will now remain underwater, just like a submarine with water in its ballast tanks.

Internet links

Go to **www.usborne-quicklinks.com** for links to the following websites:

Website 1 Information about ships, maps, navigation and the science of sailing, from historical times to the modern day.

Website 2 Take a virtual tour of a submarine and find out more about how a sub can dive and surface.

Website 3 A brief historical look at ships and their different uses.

Website 4 Take a virtual tour of an old warship and find photos of other warships at the Historic Dockyard in Portsmouth, UK.

Website 5 Explore an ancient seaport and shipyard in Connecticut, USA.

* Relative density, 41

FLIGHT

The first powered flight took place a century ago and lasted only twelve seconds. Now planes can travel faster than the speed of sound, and helicopters can hover in the air without moving. The wings of planes and the blades of helicopters have a special shape which helps them to fly.

Kites were the first things that people managed to fly.

HOW PLANES FLY

Planes can fly because of the shape of their wings. The wings are curved on top and flatter underneath. A bird's wings have the same shape. It is called an **aerofoil**.

Cross section of an aerofoil shape

Curved on top

Flow of air

Flatter underneath

★

The air above an aerofoil wing has further to travel than the air under it. When the flow of a gas such as air gets faster, its pressure is reduced. This is called **Bernoulli's principle**. Because of this, the slower air flowing under the wing has a higher pressure and pushes up on it. This force is called **lift**, and it causes the wing to rise up into the air.

Gliders are very light and the lift from their wings is strong enough to overcome the downward pull of gravity. Heavier aircraft need a force called **thrust** to stay in the air. Thrust, the force that moves a plane forwards, is provided by a plane's engines.

The more thrust an engine provides, the faster the plane goes. This greater speed improves the lift on the aircraft. The faster the wings are moving through the air, the greater the difference in air pressure above and below them.

The four forces of flight

The arrows on this picture show the four forces of flight: lift, gravity, drag and thrust.

Lift

★

Drag

Thrust

Gravity

Propellers provide thrust by pulling a plane through the air.

Jet engines provide thrust by pushing a plane through the air.

In level flight, lift is equal to the pull of gravity, and thrust is equal to drag if the speed is constant.

Drag, or **air resistance**, is another force acting on a plane. It is the force of friction* that occurs when something moves in air.

Drag increases as speed increases, so very fast aircraft are **streamlined** to reduce drag. A streamlined plane is designed so that air moves around it more smoothly.

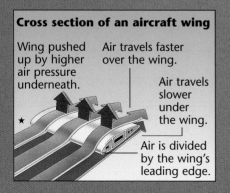

Cross section of an aircraft wing

Wing pushed up by higher air pressure underneath.

Air travels faster over the wing.

Air travels slower under the wing.

★

Air is divided by the wing's leading edge.

HOW PLANES ARE CONTROLLED

A plane needs to be able to move up and down, and to turn and bank (tip) to each side. To do this, the wings and tail are fitted with hinged flaps. These are known as **control surfaces**. They are made up of **ailerons** on the wings, and **elevators** and a **rudder** on the tail. By using a particular control surface, a pilot increases the drag on that part of the plane. This pushes it into a new position, as shown in the diagrams below.

How control surfaces work

Aileron

Rudder

Elevator

When turning, a plane also banks. This is called **rolling**. It is controlled by the ailerons on the wings.

Turning to the left or right is called **yawing**, and is controlled by the rudder on the tail fin.

Moving up and down is called **pitching**. Elevators on the tailplane control this.

See for yourself

You can create an aerofoil wing with a strip of paper 15cm x 5cm and a pencil.

Fold the strip in half with the short edges together. Then move one edge back so that it is about 1.5cm from the other edge and tape it down. This will make an aerofoil. Slide it onto a pencil, as shown.

Put the edge that hangs over the pencil close to your lips. Blow steadily over the top of the fold. The difference in air flow above and below the wing makes it rise.

Blow here.

Wing rises.

Keep blowing over top of fold.

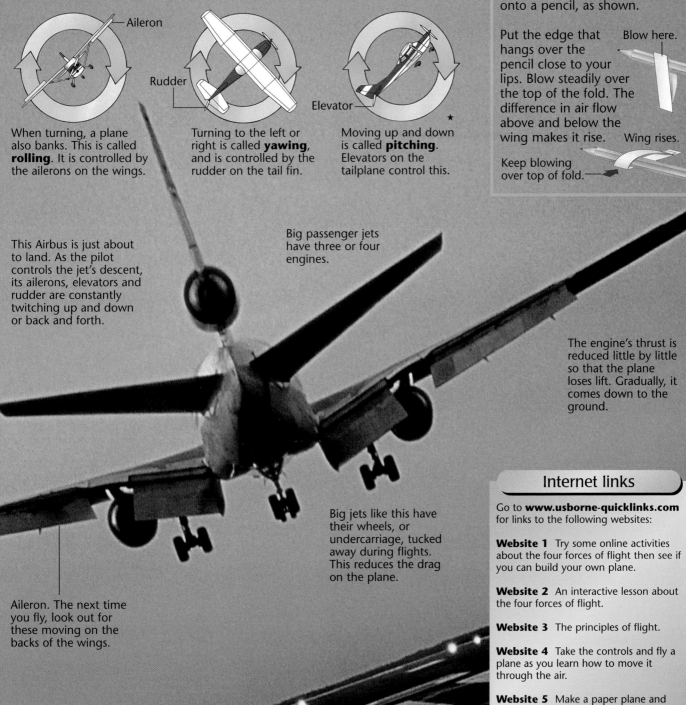

This Airbus is just about to land. As the pilot controls the jet's descent, its ailerons, elevators and rudder are constantly twitching up and down or back and forth.

Big passenger jets have three or four engines.

The engine's thrust is reduced little by little so that the plane loses lift. Gradually, it comes down to the ground.

Big jets like this have their wheels, or undercarriage, tucked away during flights. This reduces the drag on the plane.

Aileron. The next time you fly, look out for these moving on the backs of the wings.

Internet links

Go to **www.usborne-quicklinks.com** for links to the following websites:

Website 1 Try some online activities about the four forces of flight then see if you can build your own plane.

Website 2 An interactive lesson about the four forces of flight.

Website 3 The principles of flight.

Website 4 Take the controls and fly a plane as you learn how to move it through the air.

Website 5 Make a paper plane and find out about the forces that act on it.

AIRCRAFT DESIGN

The design of an aircraft depends on its function. Some planes need to be able to land on water, and some helicopters are used to lift huge weights. Here you can see some examples of different aircraft designs.

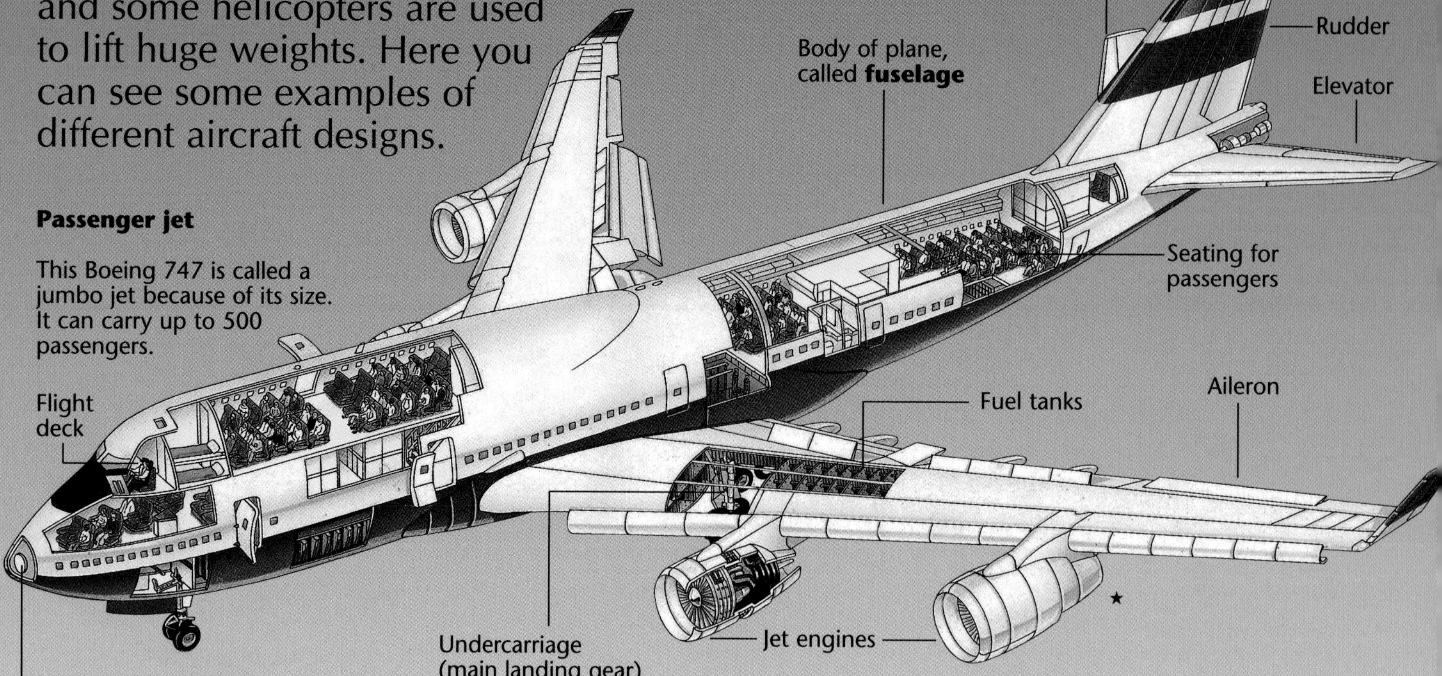

Passenger jet

This Boeing 747 is called a jumbo jet because of its size. It can carry up to 500 passengers.

Tail fin

Tailplane

Body of plane, called **fuselage**

Rudder

Elevator

Seating for passengers

Flight deck

Fuel tanks

Aileron

Undercarriage (main landing gear)

Jet engines

Radar equipment

Swing-wing plane

This Panavia Tornado is a swing-wing jet fighter. Its moveable wings can be straight (better for flying at slow speeds and landing) or swept-back (better for high-speed flying).

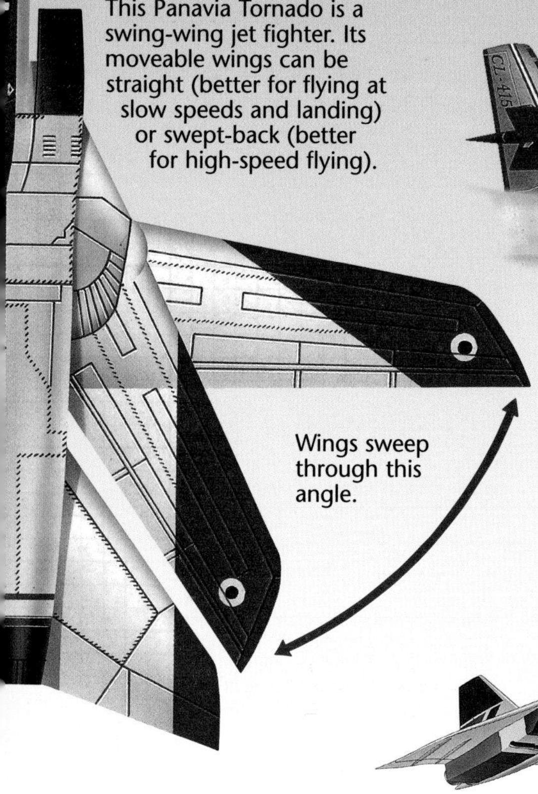

Wings sweep through this angle.

Sea plane

This Canadair CL-415 is a sea plane. It can take off and land on water. It floats because its body is shaped like a boat.

This plane also has wheels so it can move on land. Planes like this are called amphibians.

Supersonic passenger plane

Supersonic planes fly faster than the speed of sound. Concorde was the only supersonic passenger plane.

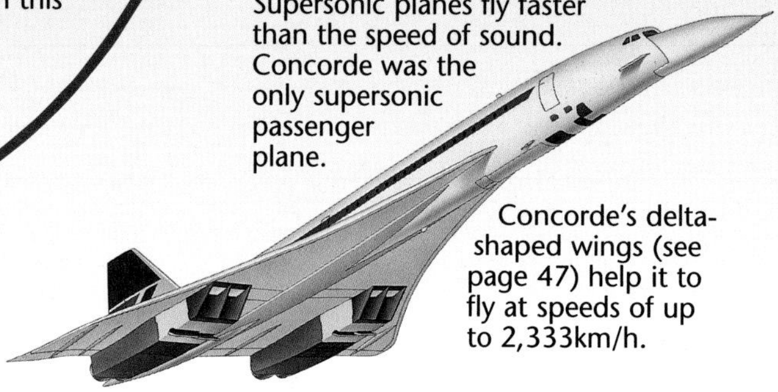

Concorde's delta-shaped wings (see page 47) help it to fly at speeds of up to 2,333km/h.

"Invisible" plane

The Northrop B2 Stealth bomber's strange "flying wing" shape helps it to avoid radar detection. It has a wingspan of over 52m.

The Stealth bomber is made of radar-absorbent materials.

Load-carrying helicopter

The Sikorsky Skycrane carries heavy loads to hard-to-reach places.

The Skycrane can carry the weight of over 150 people. Here, it is unloading a ready-made cabin to a building site.

FIRST FLIGHT

The first successful powered flight was made in 1903 by Flyer I. It was designed and built by the Wright brothers in the USA. The plane flew for about twelve seconds and lifted only a little way off the ground.

Cutaway showing wing structure

The Flyer I's wings were made of canvas stretched over a wooden frame.

HELICOPTERS

Helicopters can travel in any direction, or just hover in the air without moving. Their rotor blades are aerofoils*, which provide lift as they spin around rapidly. To provide thrust*, the blades are tilted forwards. They push the air behind them and this moves the helicopter forwards.

This Robinson R22 has two main rotor blades. Some helicopters have three or four.

The tail blades keep the helicopter stable. Without them, it would spin around. The tail blades are also used for turning.

This helicopter does not have wheels, but rests on the ground on flat blades called **skids**.

JUMP JETS

The Harrier is a **Vertical Take Off and Landing** (**VTOL**) plane, or **jump jet**. It does not need a runway to take off.

A VTOL plane has thrusters which direct the power from its jet engines. In normal flight, the thrusters point to the back. This pushes the plane forwards.

Thruster

This Harrier is taking off. Its thrusters point down at the ground, pushing the plane upwards.

WING SHAPE

How fast a plane can go depends on the shape of its wings, as well as the size of its engines.

Straight wings give enough lift* for low-speed flying, with not much drag*.

Swept-back wings reduce drag at greater speeds, and are needed for larger-sized planes, such as passenger jets.

Delta-shaped wings enable an aircraft to fly at supersonic speeds. The fastest planes use this wing shape.

See for yourself

The wings on a model plane work in the same way as on a real plane.

You can make a paper plane of your own that can do turns and stunts. For a template, plus a step-by-step guide and flying tips, go to the Web site *www.usborne-quicklinks.com* and follow the instructions.

Internet links

Go to **www.usborne-quicklinks.com** for links to the following websites:

Website 1 Find out more about the Wright brothers, with online activities.

Website 2 See how wind tunnels are used to test and design aircraft.

Website 3 Explore one hundred years of flight with lots of online activities.

Website 4 Videos, virtual tours and photographs of passenger jets.

Website 5 More commercial aircraft.

Website 6 Photographs, interactive panoramas and video clips of different types of aircraft.

* Aerofoil, Drag, Lift, Thrust, 44.

ENGINES

Engines are machines that convert the energy stored in fuel into movement. They release the energy in fuel by **combustion**, that is, by burning it. This can take place outside the engine (**external combustion**) or inside the engine (**internal combustion**).

STEAM ENGINES

The first engines were **steam engines**. They were invented about 300 years ago, and used external combustion.

In a chamber outside the engine called the **furnace**, wood or coal was burned to boil water. This produced steam. Because steam expands to take up to 2,000 times more space than water, it could be used to move a piston.

BETTER ENGINES

The earliest steam engines were not very reliable or efficient, but by the nineteenth century the technology had been improved and steam engines were being used to drive trains and power machinery in factories. James Watt (1736-1819) designed the widely-used steam engine shown here.

See for yourself

You can see the power of steam when a covered pan of water boils on a stove.

As the water boils, notice that the lid starts to bounce up and down. This is the expanding steam pushing against the lid.

Steam engines make use of this power to make things move.

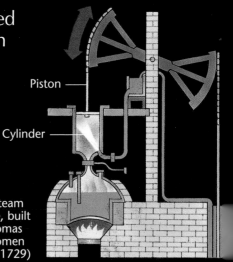

Piston

Cylinder

Early steam engine, built by Thomas Newcomen (1663-1729)

★

Pipe

James Watt steam eng

Boiler

Belt

Flywheel (5)

Cylinder (2)

Furnace (1

Condenser (3)

Sun-and-planet gear (4)

1. To make this steam engine work, coal was burned in a furnace to heat water in the boiler.

2. A pipe carried steam from the boiler to the cylinder. The steam pushed a piston up inside the cylinder.

3. The condenser took used steam from the cylinder and the piston went down. The steam turned back into water.

4. A gear called a sun-and-planet gear converted the up-and-down movement of the piston into a rotating motion.

5. The flywhe rotated to power indust machinery, to which it was connected b a belt.

TURBINES

Many modern power stations still use steam. Pressurized steam turns huge **turbines** – devices with rotating blades. This rotation generates electricity.

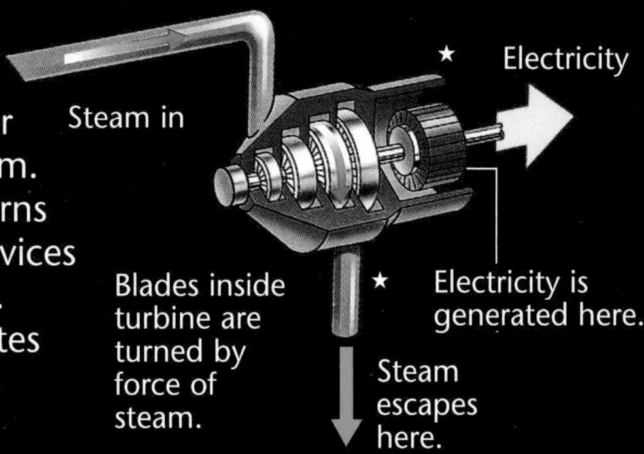

Steam in

Electricity

Blades inside turbine are turned by force of steam.

★ Electricity is generated here.

Steam escapes here.

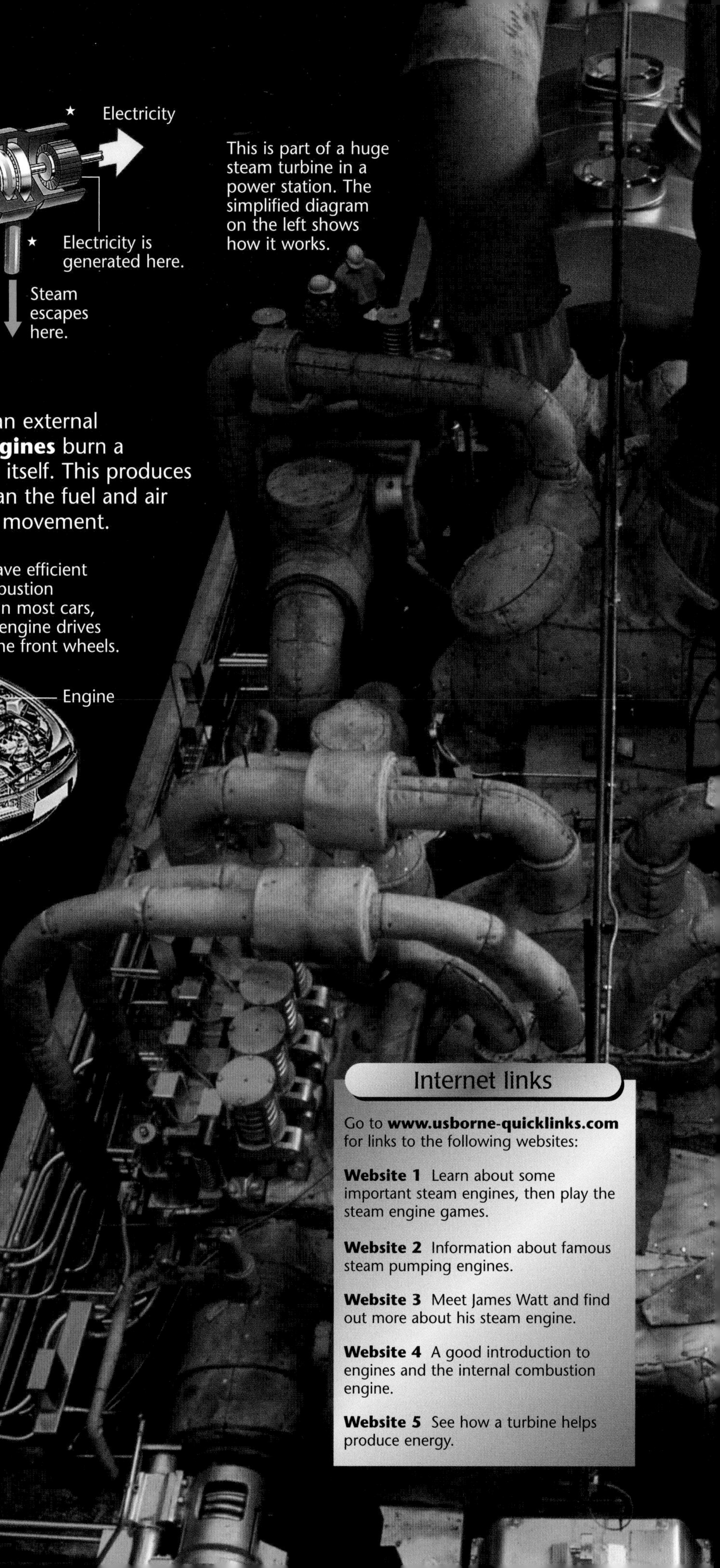

This is part of a huge steam turbine in a power station. The simplified diagram on the left shows how it works.

INTERNAL COMBUSTION

Internal combustion is more efficient than external combustion. **Internal combustion engines** burn a mixture of fuel and air inside the engine itself. This produces hot gases. These take up more space than the fuel and air they come from, and are used to create movement.

Modern cars have efficient internal combustion engines. In most cars, the engine drives the front wheels.

Engine

EXHAUST FUMES

Some of the gases produced by combustion are poisonous. They leave the engine as **exhaust fumes**.

To reduce pollution, new car engines are fitted with **catalytic converters**. These contain **catalysts**, substances that can alter the speed of chemical reactions. The converter changes the poisonous exhaust fumes into less poisonous gases.

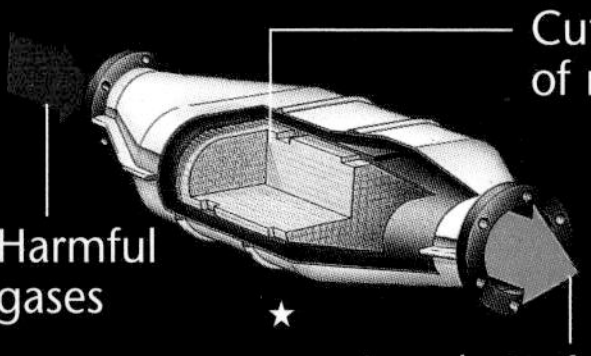

Cutaway view of metal catalyst

Harmful gases

★

Less harmful gases

In a catalytic converter, carbon monoxide is converted into carbon dioxide and water, and nitrogen oxide into nitrogen and oxygen.

Internet links

Go to **www.usborne-quicklinks.com** for links to the following websites:

Website 1 Learn about some important steam engines, then play the steam engine games.

Website 2 Information about famous steam pumping engines.

Website 3 Meet James Watt and find out more about his steam engine.

Website 4 A good introduction to engines and the internal combustion engine.

Website 5 See how a turbine helps produce energy.

PETROL ENGINES

Most car engines burn petrol. **Petrol engines** use internal combustion* to drive pistons up and down in hollow cylinders.

Each piston works in four stages called a **four-stroke combustion cycle**, as shown in the pictures on the right.

How a four-stroke engine works

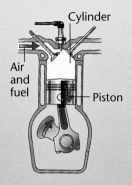

1. Piston goes down, sucking a mixture of air and fuel into cylinder.

2. Piston goes up, compressing fuel and air mixture. This heats mixture.

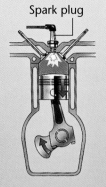

3. Spark from spark plug ignites mixture. Gases expand and force piston down.

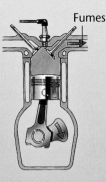

4. Piston rises again, pushing out remains of burned gases as exhaust fumes.

This is a four cylinder internal combustion car engine. It is built by Ford and called the Zetec.

Spark plug

A small spark is set off at this end of the plug.

One of the cylinders

One of the pistons

DIESEL ENGINES

Diesel fuel is used mainly by larger vehicles and some trains. **Diesel engines** work in a similar way to petrol engines, but at stroke one, only air is taken into the cylinder. This is compressed and heated to a very high temperature at stroke two. Diesel fuel is forced into the cylinder at stroke three, where it is so hot that the fuel burns without a spark.

This is the end of the crankshaft (see below).

TRANSMISSION

The four-stroke combustion cycle takes place in each of a car's cylinders. A series of shafts and gears, called the transmission, converts the up-and-down motion of the pistons into a rotating motion used to turn the wheels of the car. The system works in a similar way whether it drives the front or rear wheels of the car. (See also *Transmission* on page 53.)

Transmission system of a rear-wheel drive car

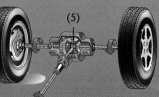

Up-and-down movement of pistons (1) turns crankshaft (2).

Gears (3) connect crankshaft to drive shaft (4).

Drive shaft turns wheels through more gears, called the differential* (5).

JET ENGINES

Jet engines are very powerful internal combustion engines* used by aircraft. The hot gases they produce are forced out of the back of the engine at high speed. This pushes the plane through the air.

Jet engines are also known as **gas turbine engines** because the hot gases turn blades called turbines in the engine. The turbines suck air into the engine and compress it before it is mixed with fuel and burned.

TURBOJET ENGINES

The **turbojet engine** below is the simplest and fastest type of jet engine. It is noisy and less efficient with fuel than a turbofan engine (see right). Turbojet engines are only used for high-speed jet planes.

Cutaway of a turbojet engine

Air enters front of engine (1). Turbines in compression chamber (2) compress air. Compressed air is channelled into combustion chamber (3) and mixed with kerosene fuel. Mixture burns and produces hot, expanding gases.

Hot gases turn another turbine (4) as they pass through back of engine. This helps to drive compression turbines near front. Gases are forced out of exhaust tailpipe (5), pushing plane forwards.

Internal combustion engines, 49.

TURBOFAN ENGINES

Turbofan engines are not as fast as turbojets, but they are quieter and use less fuel. They are fitted to passenger jets.

Cutaway of a turbofan engine

Extra large fan at front (1) sucks in huge amounts of air. Some air goes through compression and combustion chambers (2), as in turbojet, producing hot expanding gases which are forced out of back (3).

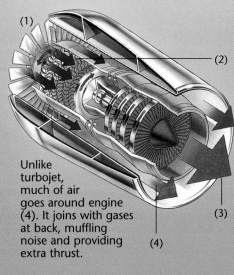

Unlike turbojet, much of air goes around engine (4). It joins with gases at back, muffling noise and providing extra thrust.

There are two other kinds of gas turbine engine:

Turboprop	Turboshaft

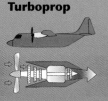

The power from the engine turns propellers that pull the plane through the air.

Turboshaft engines are usually fitted to helicopters. The engine powers the main and tail rotor blades.

ROCKET ENGINES

Like jet engines, **rocket engines** produce hot gases which are forced out at speed. Instead of sucking in air for combustion, rocket engines carry liquid oxygen. This means that they can travel in space where there is no air.

Space rockets were developed from rocket missiles, such as this V-2 made in 1942.

Rocket fuel

Liquid oxygen tank

Rocket fuel and oxygen burn in the combustion chamber.

Hot gases shoot out of the exhaust.

See for yourself

Try this to give you an idea of how jet engines work. Thread some string through a straw and tie it tightly between two pieces of furniture. Blow up a balloon and hold the end so that it doesn't deflate. Ask a friend to tape the balloon to the straw.

Now let go of the balloon. The air rushes out and the balloon shoots forwards.

Balloon

Straw — String

Internet links

Go to **www.usborne-quicklinks.com** for links to the following websites:

Website 1 Explore an interactive car and see how engines work.

Website 2 Interactive jet engine activities and a timeline of engine history.

Website 3 Take a virtual journey through a jet engine.

Websites 4-5 Compare two rockets online and watch rocket launch movies.

CARS AND MOTORBIKES

Cars, motorbikes and other road vehicles have transformed the way we live. They allow us to move from one place to another quickly and whenever we want to. But their popularity has led to problems of pollution and traffic jams. Car makers are constantly trying to develop cars that are less damaging to the environment.

This is one of the very first cars. It was built in Germany in 1885.

CAR TECHNOLOGY

The first cars were invented about 120 years ago. At first, they were slow, noisy, unreliable and dangerous. Since then, engineers and designers have refined all aspects of how cars work. These include making improvements to vital parts such as the engine, brakes, transmission and suspension. The vehicle below shows a good example of modern car design.

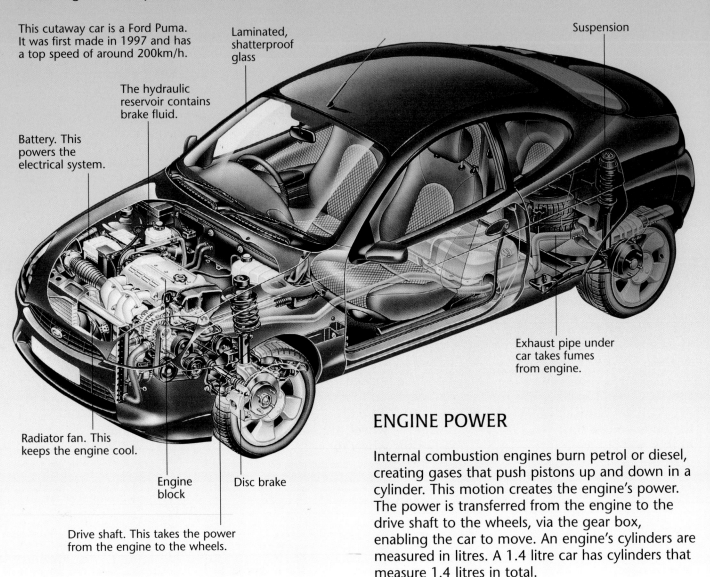

This cutaway car is a Ford Puma. It was first made in 1997 and has a top speed of around 200km/h.

Laminated, shatterproof glass

Suspension

The hydraulic reservoir contains brake fluid.

Battery. This powers the electrical system.

Exhaust pipe under car takes fumes from engine.

Radiator fan. This keeps the engine cool.

Engine block

Disc brake

Drive shaft. This takes the power from the engine to the wheels.

ENGINE POWER

Internal combustion engines burn petrol or diesel, creating gases that push pistons up and down in a cylinder. This motion creates the engine's power. The power is transferred from the engine to the drive shaft to the wheels, via the gear box, enabling the car to move. An engine's cylinders are measured in litres. A 1.4 litre car has cylinders that measure 1.4 litres in total.

*Internal combustion engines, 49.

MOTORBIKES

Motorbikes and cars share many features, although motorbikes don't need a differential (see below). Because they are relatively light, motorbikes can have engines as small as 50cm^3 (50 cubic centimetres – half a litre). Bikes with very large engines are extremely powerful and can accelerate much faster than cars.

Pillion seat

Low seat for low centre of gravity*

Petrol tank

Rear indicator

Fairing (covering) reduces drag*.

Exhaust

Suspension

Disc brake

This Honda FireBlade has a 900cm^3 engine.

Steel frame

TRANSMISSION

The **transmission** (see also page 50) is a system of **gears** that transmits an engine's power to the wheels. Gears are made of cogs (metal wheels with serrated edges called teeth). Engine power turns a rod called the input shaft, which is attached to one set of cogs. These turn another set of cogs which are attached to another rod – the output shaft. The output shaft turns drive shafts, which are attached to the wheels.

DIFFERENTIAL

The **differential** is a vital part of a car's transmission. It is a system of gears on the axles which allows the wheels to spin at different speeds. This is necessary for corners, when the outer wheels turn further and faster than the inner ones.

The inner wheel travels a shorter distance than the outer one.

★

SUSPENSION

Suspension is made up of two parts, a spring and a damper. The spring compresses and expands as the wheel goes over a bump. The damper delays the spring's action, so that the ride is not too bouncy.

The spring expands and contracts, moving a piston up and down a cylinder.

In the damper, oil is forced through valves, slowing down the piston.

★

BRAKES

Cars and motorbikes use **disc brakes**. When the brake pedal or lever is pressed, brake fluid is pushed down tubes, forcing brake pads to press against a disc in the wheel. The friction* causes the wheel to slow down.

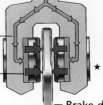

Brake fluid is forced down pipes.

Fluid pushes brake pads against the disc.

Brake disc ★

See for yourself

To see how a differential works, use two pencils, two cotton reels, a strip of paper and some tape. Roll the paper around one pencil and secure it with tape. Slide it to the blunt end and insert the other pencil. Jam the sharp end of each pencil into a cotton reel. Paint a bright spot on each pencil.

As the "wheels" turn a corner, count how many times each pencil turns.

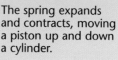

Internet links

Go to www.usborne-quicklinks.com for links to the following websites:

Website 1 See detailed explanations and animations which show how the main parts of a car work.

Website 2 Visit online museums of cars and motorcycles and see classic models from the past hundred years.

Websites 3-5 Photos, videos and details about new cars.

Website 6 An online classic car and motorsport magazine.

Website 7 Find out about the latest car technology and future innovations.

* Centre of gravity, 33; Drag, 44; Friction, 26.

UNITS OF MEASUREMENT

Measuring things is one of the most important parts of science. There are two main measuring systems: **imperial** and **metric**. The imperial system is very old, dating from the twelfth century or earlier. The metric system was introduced in France in the 1790s. This is easier to use because it is based on the system of counting in tens – the decimal system.

IMPERIAL MEASUREMENTS

Length and distance
12 inches (")	= 1 foot (')
3 feet	= 1 yard (yd)
1,760 yards	= 1 mile
3 miles	= 1 league

Area
144 square inches	= 1 square foot
9 square feet	= 1 square yard
4,840 square yards	= 1 acre
640 acres	= 1 square mile

Mass
16 drams (dr)	= 1 ounce (oz)
16 ounces	= 1 pound (lb)
14 pounds	= 1 stone
160 stone	= 1 ton

Volume and capacity
1,728 cubic inches	= 1 cubic foot (ft^3)
27 cubic feet	= 1 cubic yard (yd^3)
5 fluid ounces (fl oz)	= 1 gill (gi)
20 fluid ounces* (USA: 16)	= 1 pint (pt)
2 pints	= 1 quart (qt)
4 quarts	= 1 gallon (gal)

* UK 1 fl oz = 0.0284 litres; USA 1 fl oz (liquid) = 0.0295 litres

METRIC MEASUREMENTS

Many metric measurements are spelled ending in "re" in British English and "er" in American English; for example, "metre" and "meter".

Length and distance
10 millimetres (mm)	= 1 centimetre (cm)
100 centimetres	= 1 metre (m)
1,000 metres	= 1 kilometre (km)

Area
100 square mm (mm^2)	= 1 square cm (cm^2)
10,000cm^2	= 1 square m (m^2)
10,000m^2	= 1 hectare (ha)
100 hectares	= 1 square km (km^2)

Mass
1,000 grams (g)	= 1 kilogram (kg)
1,000 kilograms	= 1 tonne (t)

Volume and capacity
1 cubic cm (cm^3/cc)	= 1 millilitre (ml)
1,000 millilitres	= 1 litre (l)
1,000 litres	= 1 cubic metre (m^3)

Scientists usually show numbers with up to four digits closed up, without commas, for example 9999. Numbers with more digits are shown with spaces to make them easier to read, for example 0.000 001. In non-technical writing, as in this book, numbers with over three digits are shown with commas.

CONVERSIONS

To convert between metric and imperial figures, use this table with a calculator.

To convert	into	multiply by
cm	inches	0.394
m	yards	1.094
km	miles	0.621
grams	ounces	0.035
kilograms	pounds	2.205
tonnes	tons	0.984
cm^2	square inches	0.155
m^2	square yards	1.196
km^2	square miles	0.386
hectares	acres	2.471
litres	pints	1.76

To convert	into	multiply by
inches	cm	2.54
yards	m	0.914
miles	km	1.609
ounces	grams	28.35
pounds	kilograms	0.454
tons	tonnes	1.016
square inches	cm^2	6.452
square yards	m^2	0.836
square miles	km^2	2.59
acres	hectares	0.405
pints	litres	0.5683

SI UNITS

SI units (short for the French *Système Internationale d'Unités*) are an internationally agreed system of units used for scientific purposes. The units have been defined very precisely in modern times. The metre, for example, is now defined as the distance light travels in a vacuum in $1/299{,}792{,}458$ of a second. Its measurement was originally based on a length of platinum alloy kept in Paris.

Quantity	SI unit
Length	metre (m)
Mass	kilogram (kg)
Time	second (s)
Temperature	kelvin (K)
Current	ampere (A)
Amount of a substance	mole (mol)
Light intensity	candela (cd)

DERIVED SI UNITS

These are derived from the units above using the equations shown.

Quantity	Derived SI unit	Equation
Area	square metre (m²)	Depends on shape
Volume	cubic metre (m³)	Depends on shape
Density	kilograms per cubic metre (kg/m³)	$\dfrac{\text{Mass (kg)}}{\text{Volume (m}^3)}$
Velocity	metres per second (m/s)	$\dfrac{\text{Distance moved (m)}}{\text{Time taken (s)}}$
Momentum	(kg m/s)	Mass (kg) x velocity (m/s)
Acceleration	metres per second per second (m/s²)	$\dfrac{\text{Change in velocity (m/s)}}{\text{Time taken for change (s)}}$
Power	watt (W)	$\dfrac{\text{Work done (J)}}{\text{Time (s)}}$
Force	newton (N)	Mass (kg) x acceleration (m/s²)
Energy/Work	joule (J)	Force (N) x distance moved in direction of force (m)
Pressure	pascal (Pa)	$\dfrac{\text{Force (N)}}{\text{Area (m}^2)}$
Frequency	hertz (Hz)	Number of cycles per second
Electric charge	coulomb (C)	Current (A) x time (s)
Voltage	volt (V)	$\dfrac{\text{Energy transferred (J)}}{\text{Charge (C)}}$
Resistance	ohm (Ω)	$\dfrac{\text{Voltage (V)}}{\text{Current (A)}}$

TEMPERATURE SCALES

There are three main scales for measuring temperature: the Fahrenheit scale (imperial), the Celsius scale (metric) and the absolute temperature scale (SI), which is measured in kelvins.

The absolute temperature scale is seen as the most scientific because 0 kelvin (-273°C) is **absolute zero**, the temperature at which no more heat can be extracted from an object. Scientific theory holds that this point of absolute cold would be impossible to reach in practice.

Celsius (°C)	Fahrenheit (°F)	Kelvin (K)
110	230	383
100	212	373
90	194	363
80	176	353
70	158	343
60	140	333
50	122	323
40	104	313
30	86	303
20	68	293
10	50	283
0	32	273
-10	14	263
-20	-4	253
-30	-22	243
-40	-40	233
-50	-58	223
-60	-76	213
-70	-94	203
-80	-112	193
-90	-130	183
-100	-148	173
-110	-166	163

CONVERSIONS

Convert	into	calculation
°C	°F	x9,÷5,+32
°C	K	+273
°F	°C	-32,x5,÷9
°F	K	-32,x5,÷9,+273
K	°C	-273
K	°F	-273,x9,÷5,+32

FACTS AND LISTS

PHYSICAL LAWS

Here is a summary of the key physical laws, for quick reference.

Newton's first law of motion (or principle of inertia) If an object is not being acted on by a force, it will either stay still or continue moving at a constant speed in a straight line.

Newton's second law of motion Any resultant force acting on an object will change its motion. How much the motion changes depends on the object's mass and the size of the resultant force.

Newton's third law of motion When an object A exerts a force on an object B, then B exerts an equal and opposite force on A.

Newton's law of universal gravitation There is a gravitational force of attraction between any two objects with mass, which depends on the masses of the objects and the distance between them.

Archimedes' principle The upthrust acting on an object is equal to the weight of the fluid that the object displaces.

Hooke's law The extension of a material is proportional to the force stretching it.

Law of conservation of energy Energy cannot be created nor destroyed. It can only be changed into a different form.

Law of conservation of mass Matter cannot be created nor destroyed in a chemical reaction.

Law of conservation of momentum After two objects collide, their total momentum remains the same (providing no other forces are acting on them).

HALF-LIVES

The half-life of a radioactive element is the amount of time taken on average for half the nuclei in a sample to decay. Each form of an element, called an isotope, has a different half-life. This can be millions of years or under a minute. Some examples are given below.

Name	Half-life
Uranium-238	4,500,000,000 years
Iodine-129	17,000,000 years
Thorium-230	80,000 years
Plutonium-239	24,000 years
Carbon-14	5,745 years
Strontium-90	29 years
Hydrogen-3	12.3 years
Cobalt-60	5.3 years
Sulphur-35	87.9 days
Phosphorus-32	14.3 days
Iodine-131	8 days
Radon-222	3.8 days
Lead-214	26.8 minutes
Thallium-210	1.32 minutes
Radium-221	30 seconds

WEBSITES

Go to **www.usborne-quicklinks.com** for links to the following websites:

General physics

Website 1 A good source of information about many aspects of energy, forces and motion.

Website 2 A lively, illustrated study aid that covers the main areas of energy, forces and motion. Animations help understanding of major concepts.

Website 3 An online guide about science and technology, specially designed for students, that explains how physics is applied in the world today.

Website 4 Interactive, highly visual and non-technical explanations showing the laws of physics in action.

Website 5 The Institute of Physics in the UK, with the latest physics news, online activities and links.

Website 6 Animated guides that make physics easy to understand.

Website 7 A useful guide to what a physicist does and how to become one, with helpful advice and information about careers in physics.

Website 8 A searchable database of questions which have been answered by a physicist. You can also submit your own physics question.

Scientists and discoveries

Website 1 Biographies of twentieth century physicists and astronomers.

Website 2 Meet scientists, past and present, and read about their contributions to energy research.

Website 3 Visit this website for lots of facts about William Gilbert and his discovery that the Earth is magnetic.

Website 4 A fascinating online Albert Einstein exhibit, covering his formative years as well as his major discoveries.

Website 5 Lots of interesting facts about Robert Hooke and his influential work on microscopes.

Website 6 Take a look at an excellent online exhibit about Marie Curie and the science of radioactivity.

Website 7 The Nobel Prize Laureates in physics, with online games.

Website 8 Explore the world of physics with online activities and experiments for students.

Website 9 An introduction to nuclear science, including cosmic radiation.

Website 10 Innovations of the twentieth century.

SCIENTISTS AND DISCOVERIES

Ampère, André Marie (1775-1836) A French mathematician and physicist who did pioneering work on electricity and magnetism. The unit of electric current, the ampere, is named after him.

Aristotle (c.384-322BC) A Greek philosopher who made many contributions to physics, zoology and scientific theory.

Becquerel, Antoine (1852-1908) A French physicist who discovered radioactivity in 1896.

Brunel, Isambard Kingdom (1806-1859) This British engineer designed many great bridges and ocean-going steamships.

Celsius, Anders (1701-1744) This Swedish astronomer invented the first temperature scale to be divided into 100 degree units. It was named the Celsius scale.

Chadwick, James (1891-1974) An English physicist who worked on radioactivity and discovered the neutron.

Charles, Jacques (1746-1823) A French physicist who formulated Charles' law, which states the relationship between temperature and volume in gases.

Cugnot, Nicolas-Joseph (1725-1804) A French army engineer who in 1769 invented the steam tractor. This was the first vehicle to move on land by its own power.

Ford, Henry (1863-1947) An American automobile engineer who built the Ford Model T and pioneered mass-production techniques in industry.

Franklin, Benjamin (1706-1790) This American inventor and politician proved that lightning is a form of electricity.

Hooke, Robert (1635-1703) An English physicist and chemist who discovered the relationship between elasticity and force, as formulated by Hooke's law.

Joule, James (1818-1889) An English physicist who did important work on heat, and helped to establish the principle of the conservation of energy. The joule, a unit of measurement of work and energy, is named after him.

Meitner, Lise (1878-1968) This Austrian physicist explained nuclear fission for the first time in 1939. (See also *Hahn, Otto; Strassman, Fritz.*)

Newcomen, Thomas (1663-1729) An English inventor who built the first atmospheric steam engine.

Newton, Isaac (1642-1727) This English physicist and mathematician formulated fundamental laws of gravity and motion. He also discovered that light is made up of a spectrum of colours, and built the first reflecting telescope.

Pascal, Blaise (1623-1662) A French mathematician and physicist who made contributions to hydraulics and the study of atmospheric pressure. The SI unit of pressure, called the pascal, is named after him.

Röntgen, Wilhelm (1845-1923) This German physicist discovered X-rays in 1895.

Savery, Thomas (c.1650-1715) An English engineer who built the first steam engine.

Sikorsky, Igor (1889-1972) A Russian-born American aeronautical engineer who built the first successful helicopter in 1939.

Stephenson, George (1781-1848) An English inventor who invented the first successful steam locomotive in 1814 and, with his son Robert, built Stephenson's Rocket for the first passenger line in 1829.

Strassman, Fritz (1902-1980) A German chemist who, with Otto Hahn, discovered nuclear fission in 1938. (See also *Meitner, Lise.*)

Tesla, Nikola (1856-1943) A Croatian electrical engineer who invented the AC motor and high-voltage electrical generation.

Thomson, William (Lord Kelvin) (1824-1907) A British mathematician and physicist who did important work in thermodynamics, and established the absolute temperature scale.

Torricelli, Evangelista (1608-1647) An Italian physicist who devised the principle of the barometer in 1644.

Villard, Paul (1860-1934) This French physicist discovered gamma radiation in 1900.

Watt, James (1736-1819) A Scottish inventor who improved the steam engine and introduced the sun-and-planet gear. The watt, a unit of electrical power, is named after him.

Whittle, Frank (1907-1996) An English inventor who devised the jet engine in 1930.

Wright, Orville (1871-1948) and **Wilbur (1867-1912)** In 1903, these American brothers flew the first aircraft.

A-Z OF SCIENTIFIC TERMS

Absolute temperature scale The SI temperature scale, measured in kelvins (K), which are the size of degrees Celsius (°C). It places 100 kelvins between the ice point (273K) and the steam point (373K).

absolute zero The temperature at which no more heat can be removed from an object. Measured as 0K (-273°C).

acceleration A change in the velocity of an object, that is, in its speed or direction, or both per unit time.

acid rain Rain that has increased in acidity after absorbing polluting gases such as sulphur dioxide and nitrogen dioxide.

aerofoil The special wing shape, curved on top, flatter underneath, that creates lift.

aileron A control surface on a plane's wing used to direct turning and tipping (rolling).

air resistance See *drag*.

alpha particle A cluster of two protons and two neutrons emitted from the nuclei of the atoms of some radioactive substances.

alpha radiation A stream of alpha particles.

altitude Height above sea level.

atmosphere 1. The protective layer of air around the Earth that enables plants and animals to live. 2. The unit of atmospheric pressure at sea level.

atmospheric pressure The force of the air pressing down on a given area of the Earth's surface, divided by that area. At sea level, atmospheric pressure is one atmosphere (1 atm), also known as **standard pressure** and equivalent to 101,325 pascals.

atomic bomb A nuclear weapon that uses the power of nuclear fission.

atomic number The number of protons in the nucleus of an atom.

atoms The tiny particles from which elements are made. Each atom has a positively charged nucleus, consisting of protons and (except hydrogen) neutrons. This is usually balanced by enough orbiting negatively charged electrons to make the atom electrically neutral. See also *isotopes*.

Ball bearings Balls placed between two moving surfaces which reduce friction by reducing the amount of contact between the surfaces.

battery A store of chemical energy that can be converted to electrical energy.

beta particles High-energy electrons emitted when a neutron turns into a proton in the nucleus of a radioactive substance.

beta radiation A stream of beta particles.

bimetallic strip A strip made of different metals such as copper and iron fixed together, used in thermostats. When heated, the copper expands more than the iron, so the strip bends.

biogases Gases produced by rotting organic matter, used as fuel.

Calorie A unit of heat energy, equivalent to the amount of energy needed to raise the temperature of a gram of water by 1°C. It is equal to 4.2 joules. A kilocalorie, or Calorie (with a capital C), is 1,000 calories. Calories are often used instead of joules in calculations to do with energy release from food.

carbon An element found in all living things.

carbon dating A method of calculating the time that has passed since living matter died, by measuring the level of radiation from carbon-14 present in the sample. See also *isotope*; *radioisotope*.

catalyst A substance that changes the rate of a chemical reaction but is itself left unchanged.

catalytic converter A device fitted to cars which uses metal catalysts, for example platinum and rhodium, to remove toxic gases from the exhaust fumes.

Celsius scale A temperature scale which places 100 degrees Celsius (°C), between the ice point (at 0°C) and the steam point (at 100°C).

centre of gravity The point at which the whole weight of an object seems to act.

centripetal force A force that keeps an object moving in a circle.

chemical energy Energy stored in a substance and released during a chemical reaction.

combustion The scientific term for all forms of burning. It releases heat and light energy.

conduction 1. The way heat energy is transferred in a solid by the vibration of the solid's heated particles. 2. The way an electric current is transferred in a substance by the movement of free electrons.

conductor A substance through which an electric current can flow, or heat can flow easily.

contact forces Forces that require two or more objects to be touching to take effect.

control surfaces Hinged flaps on a plane's wings and tail used to control the direction of its movement.

convection The main way heat energy is transferred in fluids (liquids and gases). The part of the fluid nearest the heat source expands, becomes less dense and rises, and the denser, cooler part sinks.

convection current A movement of a liquid or gas caused by convection.

Deceleration (or **negative acceleration**) A decrease in velocity in a given time, divided by that time.

density The mass of a substance divided by its volume.

differential A part of a car's transmission which consists of gears on the axles which allow the wheels to go at different speeds.

drag (or **air resistance**) The force of friction that slows down objects moving in air.

dynamics The study of how forces affect movement.

dynamo See *generator*.

Effort The force needed to operate a machine.

elastic The term describing something that can be stretched out of shape or size by a force, but which returns to its original form when the force is removed (unless it exceeds its elastic limit). See also *plastic*.

elastic limit The point beyond which an elastic substance is altered, and weakened, permanently by stretching.

elastic potential energy (or **strain energy**) The potential energy an object has because it has been stretched or squashed.

electric charge A property of matter which causes electric forces between particles. Opposite charges attract, while like charges repel each other.

electric force The effect that electrically charged particles have on each other.

electromagnetic radiation (or **electromagnetic waves**) Energy waves made up of continually changing electric and magnetic fields, for example, light.

electron A negatively charged particle that moves round an atom's nucleus.

element A substance made up of atoms of the same type – all with the same atomic number. It cannot be broken down by a chemical reaction to form simpler substances. See also *isotopes*.

elevator A control surface on a plane's tail used to direct movement up and down (pitching).

energy chain A method, often pictorial, that shows how energy changes into different forms.

engine A machine which converts the energy stored in fuel into movement.

equilibrium The state of an object when the forces acting on it are balanced.

external combustion engine An engine which produces power from fuel burning outside its main body.

Fahrenheit scale A temperature scale which places 180 degrees Fahrenheit (°F), between the ice point (at 32°F) and the steam point (at 212°F).

field See *force field*.

fluid A liquid or gas.

force A push or pull on an object.

force field (or **field**) The area within which a force, such as a magnetic force, has an effect.

force magnifier A machine which overcomes a load greater than the effort it uses.

force ratio The load a machine needs to overcome divided by the effort.

fossil fuel A fuel such as coal, oil or natural gas, that is formed from the fossilized remains of plants or animals.

four-stroke combustion cycle The four-stage process by which the pistons in a vehicle's engine take in, compress, and ignite fuel, then release the exhaust.

frequency The number of waves passing a point in one second, measured in hertz (Hz).

friction The force that slows down moving objects that are touching.

fulcrum (or **pivot**) The fixed point around which something is turned.

fuselage The body of a plane.

Gamma radiation (**gamma rays**) Electromagnetic waves with the shortest wavelength and highest frequency. They are given off by radioactive substances.

gas turbine engine See *jet engine*.

gears A system of two or more cogs interlocking so that the motion of one controls the speed and turning effect of the other.

general theory of relativity A theory, developed by Albert Einstein, which related his special theory of relativity to gravity.

generator (or **dynamo**) A machine that converts kinetic energy into electricity.

geothermal energy Heat energy from underground rocks, used in some places to generate electricity. The rocks heat water underground, which is then pumped up and turned to steam which drives turbines.

global warming A rise in average temperatures around the world which scientists believe to be caused by the greenhouse effect.

gravitational field The area in which gravity has an effect.

gravity The pulling force that attracts objects to each other.

greenhouse effect The trapping of heat by carbon dioxide in the Earth's atmosphere.

gyroscope A wheel that spins very fast inside a freely moving frame, creating a centripetal force which enables it to tilt steeply without falling over.

Half-life The average time taken for half the radioactive atoms in a sample to decay.

hydraulic Powered by liquid pressure.

hydraulics The study of liquids in motion.

hydroelectric power Electricity generated by turbines driven by falling water.

hydrofoil A type of boat with stilts attached to underwater wings called **foils**. As it moves, the hull lifts out of the water, so water resistance is reduced.

hydrogen bomb A nuclear weapon that uses the power of nuclear fusion.

Ice point The temperature at which pure ice melts (273K; 0°C; 32°F).

inertia The tendency of objects to resist a change in their movement.

infrared radiation (**infrared rays**) Electromagnetic waves that are given out by anything hot.

instantaneous speed The speed of something at a given moment.

insulator A substance that cannot conduct electric current, or does not conduct heat well.

internal combustion engine An engine which produces power by burning fuel in an enclosed space inside.

internal energy The sum of the kinetic and potential energy of the particles in a substance.

isotopes Different forms of the same element. The atoms of each isotope have the same number of protons, but a different number of neutrons, in their nuclei. So isotopes of an element have the same atomic number, but different mass numbers. For example, carbon-12 has a mass number of 12 (and 6 neutrons in its nuclei), while carbon-14 has a mass number of 14 (and 8 neutrons).

Jet engine (or **gas turbine engine**) A powerful internal combustion engine used by aircraft. Air is sucked in through a fan, mixed with fuel and burned. The hot gas mixture turns turbine blades, and the gases are blasted out of the back of the engine at high speed.

joule (**J**) The SI unit of energy and work.

Kelvin (**K**) The SI unit of temperature. See *absolute temperature scale*.

kilocalorie (or **Calorie**) See *calorie*.

kilojoule (**kJ**) 1,000 joules.

kinetic energy The energy an object has when it is in motion.

Lift The upward force of the air flowing under an aerofoil shape such as that of an aircraft's wings.

load The force overcome by a machine.

lubricant A substance, such as oil, used to reduce friction.

Magnetism An invisible force that attracts certain metals, including iron.

mass The amount of matter contained in an object.

mass number The total number of protons and neutrons in the nucleus of an atom. The mass number of two atoms of the same element may be different, because they may be different isotopes.

millibar (**mb**) The unit of atmospheric pressure, equal to 100 pascals.

moment The turning effect of a force, measured in newton metres (Nm).

momentum A measure of an object's tendency to carry on moving, equal to its mass multiplied by its velocity.

Negative acceleration See *deceleration*.

neutron A particle with no electric charge. Neutrons form part of the nuclei of every atom (except those of hydrogen).

newton (**N**) The SI unit of force.

newton metre (**Nm**) The unit of moment.

non-renewable fuels Fuels such as coal and oil, which can be used only once (see also *renewable fuels*).

nuclear energy The energy held in the nuclei of atoms.

nuclear fission A reaction in which an atom's nucleus is split open to form two or more new nuclei, releasing large amounts of energy.

nuclear fusion A reaction in which two small nuclei are joined to form a larger one, releasing large amounts of energy.

nuclear reactor The part of a nuclear power station, or nuclear-powered vessel, in which controlled nuclear fission reactions occur.

nuclear weapons Bombs that cause devastating explosions by releasing the energy of uncontrolled nuclear reactions.

nucleus The core section of an atom that contains protons and (except hydrogen) neutrons.

Pascal (**Pa**) The SI unit of pressure, equal to a force of one newton per square metre.

photon See *quantum theory*.

piston A cylindrical part that moves up and down inside a cylinder in an engine.

pitch Of a plane, to move up or down. Pitching is controlled by the elevators.

pivot See *fulcrum*.

plastic The term used to describe a substance which does not return to its original shape after stretching, but holds its new shape instead. See also *elastic*.

pneumatic Powered by the pressure of a gas, usually air.

potential difference (or **voltage**) The work needed to push a certain amount of electric charge between two points on a conducting pathway. It is measured in volts (V).

potential energy The energy an object has because of its position in a force field such as a gravitational field.

power The rate that work is done or energy is used, measured in watts (W).

pressure The force exerted over a given area by a solid, liquid or gas.

pressurized water reactor A nuclear reactor which uses the energy from nuclear fission reactions to boil water. This makes steam that drives turbines.

proton A positively charged particle in the nucleus of an atom. The number of protons determines the element.

pulley A machine that lifts heavy loads with a system of ropes passing around grooved wheels.

Quantum theory The idea that energy comes in tiny "packets", called **quanta**, which helps to explain the properties of electrons and the relationship of energy to matter. Quanta of electromagnetic radiation, such as light, are called **photons**.

quarks Particles which are believed to make up protons and neutrons.

Radiation Energy that travels in the form of electromagnetic waves, or as high-energy particles (as emitted by radioactive substances).

radioactive decay The process by which an unstable nucleus emits radiation, becoming the nucleus of a series of different elements, until stability is reached.

radioactive tracing A medical technique used to follow a substance through a patient's body by adding radioactive elements to it.

radioactivity The release of radiation from the nuclei of unstable atoms.

radioisotope A radioactive isotope.

radiotherapy A medical technique which uses controlled doses of radiation to kill cancer cells.

relative density The density of a substance in relation to the density of water.

relative velocity The velocity a moving object appears to have when viewed from another moving object.

relativity See *general theory of relativity* and *special theory of relativity*.

renewable energy resources Sources of energy such as the Sun, wind or water, that can be used to generate power without themselves being used up (see also *non-renewable fuels*).

resultant force The total effect of all the forces acting on an object.

rocket engine An engine similar to a jet engine, but rockets carry liquid oxygen for combustion, so they can travel in space where there is no air.

rudder A control surface at the rear of ships and planes which directs turning to the left and right (yawing).

Scalar quantity A quantity that has magnitude but no direction.

SI units An internationally agreed system of standard units used for scientific measurement.

solar cell A device that converts the Sun's energy into electricity.

solar collector An array of black panels which absorbs the Sun's heat and uses it to warm water in a central heating system.

solar energy The Sun's heat and light energy.

special theory of relativity A theory, developed by Albert Einstein, which deals with the relationship of the speed of light to the measurement of time and space, and the relationship of matter to energy.

specific heat capacity The amount of heat needed to raise the temperature of 1kg of a substance by 1K.

speed The measure of how fast an object is moving, calculated as the distance it travels in a certain amount of time.

speed of light The speed at which light travels in a vacuum – about 300,000 kilometres per second.

speed of sound The speed at which sound travels – measured in dry air at 0°C as 331 metres per second.

spring balance A device which uses a spring to measure a force (in newtons).

standard pressure See *atmospheric pressure*.

steam engine The earliest kind of engine, based on external combustion, which boils water, producing steam that drives pistons.

steam point The temperature of steam above water boiling at atmospheric pressure (373K; 100°C; 212°F).

strain energy See *elastic potential energy*.

streamlining A way of designing vehicles so that air flows over them in smooth lines, reducing drag.

supersonic speed Any speed greater than the speed of sound.

suspension A system of springs in a vehicle that absorbs the effects of an uneven road surface.

Terminal velocity The maximum velocity reached by a falling object, at which point acceleration ceases, and velocity is constant.

thermal capacity The amount of heat needed to raise the temperature of an object by one kelvin.

thermodynamics The study of energy changes involving heat.

thermostat A device that switches an electric circuit on and off in response to a change in temperature. See also *bimetallic strip*.

thrust The force that moves a plane or rocket forwards.

transmission A system of gears that transmits the engine's power to the wheels of a vehicle.

turbine A machine with a shaft and blades, which are turned, for example, by the force of wind or steam. The movement (kinetic) energy is converted into electricity.

turbofan engine A type of jet engine with an extra-large fan. They are slower than turbojets, but quieter and more efficient.

turbojet engine The fastest type of jet engine, used in high-speed jet planes.

turboprop engine A jet engine that drives propellers to power an aircraft.

turboshaft engine A jet engine that powers the rotor blades in a helicopter.

Upthrust The force of a fluid pushing up on an object inside it.

Vacuum An empty space where there are no particles of air or other matter.

vector quantity A quantity that has magnitude and direction.

velocity The speed an object travels in a particular direction.

voltage See *potential difference*.

volume The amount of space an object occupies.

VTOL Of a plane, Vertical Take Off and Landing. Such planes take off directly upwards and so do not need runways.

Watt (**W**) The SI unit of power.

weight A measure of the strength of the pull of gravity on an object.

work Work is done when a force moves an object. It involves a transfer of energy and is measured in joules. One joule equals the work done when a force of one newton moves an object one metre.

Yawing Of a plane or ship, turning to the left or right. It is controlled by the rudder.

TEST YOURSELF

1. Energy is measured in units called
A. watts
B. joules
C. kilograms   *(Page 12)*

2. The boiling point of water is
A. 32°F
B. 100°C
C. 212°C   *(Page 13)*

3. Which statement is true?
A. convection never occurs in solids
B. convection only occurs in liquids
C. conduction never occurs in solids   *(Pages 14-15)*

4. An alpha particle is made up of
A. two protons and two neutrons
B. two protons
C. a high-speed electron   *(Page 16)*

5. Radioactive carbon-14 is written as $^{14}_{6}C$. This form of carbon has
A. six protons and six neutrons
B. six protons and eight neutrons
C. fourteen protons   *(Page 17)*

6. A force's strength is measured in
A. kilograms
B. metres
C. newtons   *(Page 21)*

7. A force is
A. a vector quantity
B. a scalar quantity
C. neither a vector nor a scalar quantity   *(Page 21)*

This digram shows the forces acting on a wheelbarrow.

Which arrow represents

8. the force of the ground on the wheelbarrow?   *(Page 23)*

9. the force of the man on the wheelbarrow?   *(Page 23)*

10. the weight of the wheelbarrow?   *(Page 23)*

11. It is easier to turn something around a fulcrum if the force is applied
A. a long distance from the fulcrum
B. very close to the fulcrum
C. at the fulcrum   *(Page 23)*

12. If no forces are acting on a moving object, the object will
A. slow down and stop
B. continue moving at the same speed in a straight line
C. change direction   *(Page 24)*

13. Whenever you push an object you will always feel
A. a push in the opposite direction
B. a push in the same direction
C. no push at all   *(Page 24)*

14. When a book slides across a table, the force that slows it down is called
A. lubrication
B. drag
C. friction   *(Page 26)*

15. Average speed is equal to
A. distance multiplied by time
B. time divided by distance
C. distance divided by time   *(Page 28)*

16. The difference between speed and velocity is that
A. speed is a scalar quantity whereas velocity is a vector quantity
B. speed is a vector quantity whereas velocity is a scalar quantity
C. they have different units   *(Page 29)*

17. If an object accelerates, then its
A. speed and direction must change
B. speed or direction must change
C. speed must increase   *(Page 29)*

18. An apple falling from a tree is pulled downwards because of
A. the pull of gravity on the apple
B. the apple's low centre of gravity
C. the smooth skin of the apple, which reduces friction   *(Page 32)*

19. Which statement is true?
A. the mass of an object depends on the pull of gravity on that object
B. mass is measured in newtons
C. the weight of an object is due to the pull of gravity of the Earth on that object   *(Pages 32-33)*

20. Which statement is true?
A. a force acting over an area exerts pressure
B. the pressure of a needle is small due to the small area of the point
C. hydraulic machines are driven by gas pressure   *(Pages 34-35)*

21. Atmospheric pressure
A. is at its lowest near to the ground
B. increases with height above ground
C. is due to the weight of air pressing down   *(Page 34)*

22. When using a lever
A. the point about which the lever turns is called the fulcrum
B. the force you apply is the load
C. the force you need to overcome is called the effort   *(Page 36)*

23. Which statement is correct?
A. a man doing work gains energy
B. work is only done when a force makes an object move
C. work and power are both measured in watts   *(Page 39)*

24. Ships made of steel float because
A. steel is less dense than water
B. the hollow space inside the ship makes it less dense than water
C. the upthrust of the water on the ship is less than the weight of the ship   *(Page 41)*

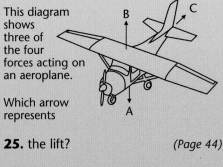

This diagram shows three of the four forces acting on an aeroplane.

Which arrow represents

25. the lift?   *(Page 44)*

26. the aeroplane's weight? *(Page 44)*

27. the drag?   *(Page 44)*

28. In the diagram above, the missing force is the
A. pull of the Earth's gravity
B. thrust provided by the engines
C. centripetal force   *(Page 44)*

29. In level flight, lift is equal to the
A. speed of the aeroplane
B. pull of gravity
C. air resistance   *(Page 44)*

30. Wings that are curved on top and flatter underneath are called
A. hydrofoils
B. aerofoils
C. ailerons   *(Page 44)*

Answers

1.B 2.B 3.A 4.A 5.B 6.C 7.A 8.A 9.C 10.B 11.A 12.B 13.A 14.C 15.C 16.A 17.B 18.A 19.C 20.A 21.C 22.A 23.B 24.B 25.B 26.A 27.C 28.B 29.B 30.B

61

INDEX

You will find the main explanations of terms in the index on the pages shown in bold type. It may be useful to look at the other pages for further information.

WEBSITES

ACKNOWLEDGEMENTS

PHOTO CREDITS
(t = top, m = middle, b = bottom, l = left, r = right)

Corbis: **2-3** Richard T. Nowitz; **6-7** Joseph Sohm, ChromoSohm, Inc; **10-11** Sean Aidan, Eye Ubiquitous; **14-15** (main) Gary Braasch; **17** (b) Owen Franken; **18-19** (main) Bettmann; **21** (main) Robert Landau; **49** (main) Richard Hamilton Smith.
© **Digital Vision**: **1**; **4-5**; **8** (t), (b); **9** (bl); **12** (l); **14** (l), (bm); **15** (tr); **19** (ml); **20** (tr); **22**; **25** (tm), (tr); **26**; **28** (t), (br); **30** (t), (b); **34** (tr), (bl); **40-41** (t); **42-43**; **44-45**.
NASA: **27** (l)
Science Photo Library: **32** (b) Science Photo Library;
35 (tr) Will & Deni McIntyre; **37** (main) Jeremy Walker.
Ford Motor Co Ltd 27 (tr); **36** (r); **49** (ml); **50** (m); **52-53**;
Goodyear GB Ltd 26 (l); **Honda UK 53** (tr); **Northern Lites 34** (m);
Porsche Cars Great Britain 29 (bm); **Snow and Rock 26** (br).
Tony Stone: **cover** Robin Smith

ILLUSTRATORS
Simone Abel, Sophie Allington, Rex Archer, Paul Bambrick, Jeremy Banks, John Barker, Andrew Beckett, Joyce Bee, Stephen Bennett, Mark Bergin, Roland Berry, Gary Bines, Isabel Bowring, Trevor Boyer, John Brettoner, Peter Bull, Hilary Burn, Andy Burton, Terry Callcut, Kuo Kang Chen, Stephen Conlin, Sydney Cornfield, Dan Courtney, Steve Cross, Gordon Davies, Peter Dennis, Richard Draper, Brin Edwards, Wayne Ford, John Francis, Mark Franklin, Nigel Frey, Stephen Gardener, Peter Geissler, Nick Gibbard, William Giles, David Goldston, Peter Goodwin, Jeremy Gower, Teri Gower, Terry Hadler, Alan Harris, Nick Hawken, Nicholas Hewetson, Christine Howes, John Hutchinson, Ian Jackson, Hans Jessen, Karen Johnson, Richard Johnson, Elaine Keenan, Frank Kennard, Aziz Khan, Stephen Kirk, Richard Lewington, Brian Lewis, Jason Lewis, Steve Lings, Rachel Lockwood, Kevin Lyles, Chris Lyon, Kevin Maddison, Janos Marffy, Andy Martin, Josephine Martin, Rob McCaig, Joseph McEwan, David McGrail, Malcolm McGregor, Dee McLean, David Mead, Annabel Milne, Robert Morton, Louise Nevet, Martin Newton, Louise Nixon, Steve Page, Justine Peek, Maurice Pledger, Mick Posen, Russell Punter, David Quinn, Barry Raynor, Mark Roberts, Michael Roffe, Michelle Ross, John Russell, Michael Saunders, John Scorey, John Shackell, Chris Shields, David Slinn, Guy Smith, Peter Stebbing, Stuart Trotter, Robert Walster, Craig Warwick, Ross Watton, Phil Weare, Hans Wiborg-Jenssen, Sean Wilkinson, Ann Winterbottom, Gerald Wood, David Wright, Steve Wright.